To Muriel,

Neither Success nor M
tarry among the Unprepared.

Praise for *The Prepared Investor*

"Manske is innovative, a clear communicator, and an excellent storyteller. I highly recommend his book to anyone experiencing concern about current events affecting their financial future."

—HAZEM AHMED, EXECUTIVE VICE PRESIDENT
FOR INDEPENDENT BANK

"Being prepared for when plans go awry is an important part of goal accomplishment. You can't be a thinking person today and be unaware of the potential for future crisis. I give Manske's book two thumbs up!"

—MIKE FEINBERG, PRESIDENT OF THE TEXAS SCHOOL VENTURE
FUND, CO-FOUNDER OF KIPP, AND RECIPIENT OF AN HONORARY
DOCTORATE OF HUMANE LETTERS FROM YALE UNIVERSITY

"Manske reminds us of that which matters most. We can persevere, we can overcome. Chris brings a unique presence to his work, which you feel as you read this book. We are right to hope, and we have more control over our financial independence than Wall Street typically suggests."

—DR. BOB STECKER, ELDER-IN-RESIDENCE AND SUBJECT OF *LIFE
LESSONS FROM THE OLDEST & WISEST* BY DAVID ROMANELLI

"I manage approximately $70 million for a variety of institutional and personal clients. Manske's book is relevant and a must-read for any investment advisor who gets asked about how a future crisis will affect financial independence."

—ZACH WELBORN, INVESTMENT ADVISOR
AND CERTIFIED FINANCIAL PLANNER

"Manske is one of those people whose words are as powerful as his presence. I've seen him speak in a ballroom filled with business owners and sales professionals. He's an excellent communicator with something very relevant to say. Read his book!"

—DAVID R. BREWER, MANAGING PARTNER AT THE BREWER LAW FIRM, PRESIDENT OF FIDELITY NATIONAL TITLE, FOUNDING MEMBER OF THE INDUSTRY MASTER'S FORUM, AND SUMMA CUM LAUDE GRADUATE OF PRINCETON UNIVERSITY

"Part investing, part history, all positive. Manske gives a clear statement about the tenacity and optimism that can accompany the worst crisis."

—MAX C. LUMMIS, CPA, CFE, CVA, PRINCIPAL CONSULTANT AT LCS FORENSIC ACCOUNTING & ADVISORY

"I admire Manske's honesty, determination, and well-researched approach as he tells the world that the typical dogma surrounding crisis investing is just the tip of the iceberg. Highly recommended!"

—PAMELA O'BRIEN, PRINCIPAL DESIGNER AT PAMELA HOPE DESIGNS

"I am proud to have been involved early on with Manske's project based on interest from some of my contacts when I mentioned the book. This is a very meaningful work by a topnotch financial professional. It is concise, with original concepts, and takes the reader down a logical path."

—CHARLES G. FERTITTA, JR., PRINCIPAL & DIRECTOR AT COLLIERS INTERNATIONAL

THE
PREPARED
INVE$TOR

How to Prevent the Next Crisis from Affecting Your Financial Independence

CHRISTOPHER R. MANSKE

CHANGING LIVES PRESS

Published by
Changing Lives Press
P.O. Box 140189 • Howard Beach, NY 11414
www.changinglivespress.org

ISBN: 978-0-99043-966-0

Library of Congress Cataloging-in-Publication Data is available through the Library of Congress.

Edited by: Michele Matrisciani • https://michelem.net
Cover and interior by Gary A. Rosenberg • www.thebookcouple.com

Printed in the United States of America

10   9   8   7   6   5   4   3   2   1

Contents

For those who,
like Atlas,
carry much for others

Introduction

"I'm just not going to look at my investments. They say I need to hold on. They say it will pass. But this is once in a lifetime! It's unprecedented! I'm not going to sell, that's for sure! Just give it time; someday it will come back. I'll just work a little longer if I have to. Everyone is going through it; I'm not alone. I can hold up my end of the bargain. Bad times don't last forever; I'll just keep my head down and do like everyone else until things clear up."

—FINANCIAL CRISIS, 2008

"No one could have predicted this. It's such a tragedy. Anyone who says they saw this coming is just trying to sell something. It's affecting so many people! I've lost so much money, so what's going to happen now? Nothing is ever going to be the same, is it?"

—TECHNOLOGY BUBBLE, 2000

"How will I get through this with my financial future intact? My money has been dropping and I've watched my portfolio shrink; I just need to stop the bleeding. What if it keeps dropping? What if I lose it all? This has never happened! It's totally new! Everyone's afraid. Maybe I should just sell so I can't lose any more."

—9/11 TERRORIST ATTACK, 2001

"This is unprecedented—we've never seen this before. No one knows what to expect because it's all so new, so scary. No one knows what to do. All the news talks about is fallout and unknown consequences. It's the worst we've ever seen! Everywhere I look on social media, it's clear we're all in for an extremely difficult time ahead. How are we going to get through this?"
—COVID-19 QUARANTINE, 2020

There's a typical Wall Street response to any and all crises, including the ones above: keep your diversified portfolios in place, and someday, maybe years from now, investments will return to where they once were. The typical Wall Street investment advisor will remind us that bad things have happened before. They'll say, "It will affect us temporarily, but you need to hold on. Someday, maybe years later, markets will recover and we will have put that tragedy behind us." They'll add, "Your portfolio won't disappear, but of course it will be affected. Everyone will be affected. You might have to tighten things up a bit, but it won't be the end of the world. Take the long view and everything will be okay. We'll get through it together."

This type of wait-it-out mentality implies that there is no way at all to prepare. It suggests that, in the face of crisis, you are completely out of control without any action available to move you financially ahead. How has the majority of the investing public accepted this for so long?

The just-hold-on approach has survived to become Wall's Street's main answer to crisis investing for three reasons. First, it works, albeit inefficiently. Just like a stopped clock will tell the right time if we wait long enough, the vast majority of portfolios will rise again someday to surpass historical high values. Second, investors often feel comforted by this approach. We all feel a little more secure knowing that we're not alone and that we're hanging on alongside everyone else. Misery loves company and the wait-and-see approach capitalizes on this. The third reason there's a one-size-fits-all approach to crisis rests on the principle that "easy" sells better than "complicated." It's such a basic concept, anyone can get it. All you have to do is nothing. Let time fix the problem.

This tradition of patience and wait-it-out isn't altogether a terrible approach because, sure, given enough time, the markets do come around, but at what expense? Could you have gained while others were losing? Do you have years to wait when your income stream relies on your portfolio today? By doing nothing to prepare, how many more years of work are you accepting before you can retire? Could you have more money to spend each month later in life? There is a future you, an older person you've yet to meet, who will look back on the choices you're making right now and wonder, "Why did I wait all that time to take action when I could have been prepared? If I could have recognized the opportunities within the crisis to protect and grow my portfolio, why did I do nothing?"

No one wakes up magically prepared for calamity. Preparation is an intentional act requiring education, resolve, and pattern recognition. When you are prepared, you experience less fear, engage in more grounded decision-making, and exit the crisis far better off than those who did nothing. Procedurally, preparing for the next major financial crisis is no different from anticipating any problem such as a broken water pipe in winter or a flat tire on a lonely road. When I taught my teenage daughter how to change a tire, it took some resolve to set the time aside and provide her that education. Her training wasn't only focused on what to do after the tire is flat; it also focused on pattern recognition and cause-and-effect exercises. For example, if you don't have a jack and a tire iron, then you won't be able to fix your flat tire, so get the equipment and keep it in your trunk. If you mindlessly drive into potholes, the probability of getting a flat is greater. Because the chance of getting a flat increases with bald tires, checking your tire air pressure and treads is a habit worth developing. Preparing for that future flat tire requires foundational work like education on how your equipment lifts the car and learning the importance of staying calm as the traffic roars by your parked vehicle.

When the next flat tire strikes, could my daughter just stand there on the side of the road? Could she just do nothing and wait? Sure, she could, but it's not the optimal strategy. At some point, someone might come along who will offer her a ride. Maybe she stands there an hour, maybe all day. Doing nothing isn't bad or wrong; it's just not going to efficiently get her back on the road. Some of the teenagers my daughter knows have shared that, in their opinion, cell phones mean they don't need to learn how to change a tire. They aren't wrong. They just aren't prepared.

Being prepared starts with accepting that certain things happen over and over. My phone inevitably will run out of juice so I plug it in each night. That simple act of preparedness ensures I have the use of my cell phone all day. I have a protective case around my cell phone because I've accepted that I may occasionally drop it. My wife keeps an umbrella in the car because, one time, she was caught in the rain and, when she got soaked, it derailed her whole day.

Preparation is not predicting the future. If I get a call and learn that my daughter has a flat tire, it will be a surprise. I couldn't predict she'd have a flat at that time, in that weather, on that road, on the way to that important appointment. And the next time she gets a flat tire, it will be just as much a surprise. That second flat will assuredly be in different weather, on a different road, and on her way to a different appointment. But the work she does as a driver, ahead of each flat, is the same. And the work she does once the crisis hits is extremely similar despite the changing details of how the flat occurred. If she's headed to a formal dinner, she might focus more on protecting her clothing from dirt and grime. If her tire goes flat on a hill, she'll need to seriously examine how to lift the car safely on the incline.

Preparation doesn't remove the element of surprise, but my daughter's knowledge and feeling of being prepared for a flat, even if the chances are slim, lowers the elements of risk and loss. Being prepared means she's sure to spend less time stuck on the side of the road. A quicker turnaround means less exposure to a lot of other unknowns that might happen on the roadside and could lead to worse problems that are harder to imagine or predict.

Preparation in the Financial World

Picture a world where people don't keep spare tires because they plan to just stand on the side of the road waiting for something or someone to come along who helps them get going again. Sounds crazy, right? Yet that is exactly what most people do in times of crisis with their investment portfolios. The prevailing approach to financial crisis is to wait it out. At some point, maybe years later, the portfolio will be back to where it once was. But this waiting game isn't a prepared response, like staying calm on the side of the road, changing the tire, and being on time to an appointment. When crisis happens, the passive approach of waiting exposes your financial future to irrational fear, panic, and counterproductive behaviors—the opposite of preparation.

Imagine a scenario where multiple people get a flat tire at the same time in the same place. The one person who had prepared for this emergency is back on the road before the vast majority of other drivers. What's more, the road is mostly empty now because so many people are standing on the shoulder of the highway waiting for help. This means the prepared driver will reach the destination faster. When the next crisis strikes, the strategies provided in the pages ahead will enable you to do more than just get back on the road; it will accelerate you ahead of other investors. Becoming a Prepared Investor means you will be able to calmly protect, and even grow, your net worth in the face of crisis.

This book and the perspectives within it are a culmination of more than twenty years' investment acumen built on a decade of military experience that began at the U.S. Military Academy at West Point. Training and preparation have been the bedrock for much of my success, whether it was being selected by Merrill Lynch to train thousands of financial advisors nationwide or serving more than 100,000 employees as the lead financial advisor within the University of Texas Employee Assistance Program. Today, I run my own firm leading a disciplined and well-credentialed team that provides sophisticated wealth management for hundreds of millions of dollars. We offer individualized investment advice to clients all over the world, always with preparation in mind as we examine their specific goals and future requirements.

At its core, *The Prepared Investor* is about cause and effect. Just as a flat tire will make a car difficult to drive, specific catalysts create certain patterns of behavior. In the pages ahead, you'll learn that the more a crisis is new and threatening, the easier it is to recognize the familiar response. *The Prepared Investor* is a call to action to stop patterns of avoidance, passivity, and wait-and-see that my team and I have found detrimental and unnecessary to individuals' personal growth strategies. The signals, patterns, and behavioral approaches in this book can help you prepare to answer the question, "How can I protect and grow my net worth despite the results of the next crisis?"

The general consensus of panic, confusion, and erratic behavior when it comes to managing crisis and personal wealth implored me to write this book. Over the years and through multiple crises, my team and I have addressed many different fears and critical questions, including:

- "If there's a terrorist attack, how will my portfolio do?"

- "What if the quarantine is never fully lifted? Is my portfolio ever going to come back?"

- "If the United States gets involved in a war, is my financial independence secure?"

- "I know peace won't last forever; something bad is going to happen. As my investment advisor, are we ready for that?"

In the chapters ahead, I'll show you that crisis, in general, happens all the time without affecting the stock market. Understanding the difference between simple catastrophe and a disaster accompanied by a financial, fear-based reaction will arm you with the skills needed to take the right steps to ensure the crisis doesn't dictate your personal wealth management decisions. After reading this book, you will be in a better position to protect and grow your net worth rather than joining the unprepared drivers on the side of the road who don't even have a spare tire.

Each chapter provides specific action steps you can use to financially prepare for the next crisis and the historical details to support them. With the benefit of hindsight, I'll deconstruct major historical episodes such as wars, terrorist attacks, novel viruses, and terrible weather events to illustrate how, while each crisis varied, the fear reaction was ultimately the same. The circumstances, the locations, and the cultural norms regarding these historical episodes were different, but the basic challenge to the investment markets remained eerily similar.

There is wisdom in understanding historical patterns and predictable responses. Over the years, the stock market has served as a giant data pool, allowing us to draw parallels and find congruity in the ways investors have responded to crisis. With this type of examination, we can follow trends, see patterns, and understand how people will come to respond and react in the marketplace. In fact, throughout the book, I have included charts to graphically show the way the market moved in each crisis to help drive home the point that the next catastrophe will look very similar regardless of the date and details. Big-picture understanding of human behavior and financial turbulence helps the Prepared Investor avoid being completely subjected to the whims of the collective fear response. The ideas within this book will change your viewpoint and make you hyperaware of how the market will respond in the future because you will be informed by the commonality of the past.

As you read about how people have impulsively reacted when they could've been thoughtful and pragmatic, you'll begin to learn the predictable signs that indicate society is behaving instinctually (reaction) instead of rationally (response) when it comes to their financial future. The Prepared Investor is one who notices patterns, understands human behavior, isn't prone to following the conventions of the masses, and responds accordingly. The pages ahead offer you twenty action steps I've developed over thirty years in both the military and financial service. Tempered by hundreds of hours of third-party research and professional feedback, each step is an important part of your journey to being financially prepared for the next disaster. Behind the data, there are many stories of humanity to help contextualize the strategies of *The Prepared Investor*.

Whether you feel the world is experiencing Armageddon or you just want to be ready for the next major crisis, preparation starts with education. Once you're aware of the various types of crises that affect portfolios and the patterns that result, you can respond in a way that better protects your financial future. No one can say exactly when the next crisis will be, but we know that another one is coming. It's this knowledge that you and I share, this certainty that tomorrow will have its challenges, that has put my book in your hands. *The Prepared Investor* is designed to be a meaningful training tool, reminding us that we don't need to sit on the side of the road watching traffic go by. Tomorrow's unknown crisis is not something to avoid in fear. It requires our attention and deliberation. We just need to have the courage to face the truth of our future's uncertainty. We just need to be prepared.

CHAPTER ONE

All Crises Are Not Created Equal:
Two Types of Crisis
That Affect the Stock Market

"**M**y neighbor is worried about some kind of dirty bomb that knocks out our internet and electricity. He's stocking up on supplies, and I think he wants to buy a bunker or something. I guess it's just a matter of time until something happens, right? What if I've just retired when crisis hits? How will I continue to live comfortably? I'm not going to bury gold in my backyard, but I do want to be reasonably prepared."

This is part of a conversation I had years ago on the phone with a client. I've spent almost twenty years circling this topic with people all over the country, and I've answered some variation of these questions for both investors and the Wall Street advisors who guide them. These issues arise because it's impossible for anyone keeping up with current events to believe that the future will be completely free of problems. It's so easy for investors to see an uncertain future, they feel pressure to do something about it. People know, deep down, that it is not responsible to just sit, completely unprepared, in the face of such clear instability. People can tell they are unprepared, and, when they start conversations like this one, they hope to do something about it.

Almost all of these discussions start with a legitimate worry. Terrorists could attack our electrical system. What if something like the Tech Bubble happens again? North Korea has nukes. What if a serious virus threatens to wipe out a large portion of the population?

Political tension among leaders keeps escalating both domestically and abroad. Is the 2008 Financial Crisis really over yet? Russia is interfering in our elections. What if they fly a plane into a skyscraper? What will happen to my money? How will it affect my future? What can I do in the face of crisis to protect and grow my portfolio?

Such questions are not unique. Over time and across many different situations, the questions stay the same and the worry rarely wanes. That's because the answer to the questions has been so incomplete. We're told to do nothing. You can't predict the next downturn, so don't bother to prepare yourself. Take the easy path and just wait it out. Let's see what happens. Someday, the market will come back.

It's time to change the investing-through-crisis conversation. Both investment professionals and the clients they serve know that the typical wait-it-out approach is not complete. There's much more to this story that's hidden from view. If we dig deeper, we find that all crises are not created equal, and therefore, our responses shouldn't be equal. The type of crisis matters and greatly determines how investors will react. Therefore, the question becomes, "How can I classify and recognize the serious crises that will affect my personal wealth and future growth decisions?" To accomplish this, we must first set aside what does *not* constitute an immediate crisis for your investment portfolio.

Not a Crisis

Comedians like Louis C.K. and George Carlin have ridiculed society for watering down the definition of certain words and using them too much. For better or worse, the word "crisis" falls into this clichéd category. In the years it's taken me to research and write this book, I've found it interesting that people often define "crisis" so broadly. (For some, the fact that the stock market does not always go up is itself a crisis.)

The older I get, the more I respect that different people have different personal thresholds for calamity. For example, someone may be sincerely distraught to be caught wearing the wrong attire at a friend's party. Someone else may laugh at that but be terribly affected when they are late to an appointment. Whether or not these individual difficulties are a crisis, we can agree that they will not move the stock market.

However, there are other, more serious, crises that also will not meaningfully affect your investments. The daily news is full of these disasters, yet I've never had to talk with clients about them. Why is it that no one has ever asked me, "If an ambulance gets a flat tire on an important trip in Cincinnati, how will that affect my portfolio?" No one has ever said to me, "I'm worried about the next tornado that sweeps through Oklahoma. How is that going to affect my portfolio?" I've never gotten a flood of calls from worried clients after a truck driver fell asleep at the wheel in North Carolina.

Certainly, each of these three examples are terrible occurrences that we'd all prefer not ever happen. Even so, people naturally recognize that situations like a tired truck driver having an accident don't affect the broad investing markets. They understand there's very little connection between these troubling events and a drop in the stock market. But they don't know *why*. They assume that the *size* of the crisis determines whether or not investors will negatively react and cause the stock market to go down.

Mistakenly seeing the locality of an event, the vast majority of Wall Street professionals and Main Street shareholders would agree that a fatigued trucker's accident in North Carolina doesn't create much financial uncertainty in the broad markets. But let's change this truck driver into a very specific man who, in March 2006, was consumed with hurting any and all Americans as part of a religious ideology. This was a time in history when the United States had little experience with a vehicle being maliciously used as a weapon. The driver, now known terrorist, Mohammed Taheri-azar, drove into a group of students at the University of North Carolina at Chapel Hill. No one was killed, but nine were injured. The stock market dropped in reaction even though it's the same truck in the same town doing the same damage as our starting example with the tired driver.

11

The size or deadliness of a crisis is immaterial to the question of whether or not the stock market will be affected. The two major criteria that help predict when a stock market panic may ensue are:

1. If the crisis is new and unknown.

2. If people feel a connection (real or not) to the danger.

People don't ask me if the ambulance in Cincinnati or the truck driver in North Carolina will affect the stock market because they are only thinking of size, which has little to do with it. Big or small, if it's not a new and scary threat, then the crisis will likely fail to significantly impact investors in the short term.

ACTION STEP #1: Identify the two types of crisis that affect the stock market: threatening and systemic.

Threatening Crisis

From an investor's point of view, new and scary threats can be categorized into two types of crises: threatening and systemic. A threatening crisis brings people together and creates consensus. There's very little controversy or subjectivity when we are in danger or feel threatened. Threats create an empirical reaction and therefore a predictable one. Throughout history, the one catalyst that motivates humans to set aside the smaller differences and the daily distractions is a threatening one. The momentary belief that someone or something is out to harm us aligns our perspectives in a very powerful, albeit temporary, way. For this reason, the majority of this book focuses on how to protect and grow your portfolio in the face of this kind of disaster. A threatening crisis involves intent and can almost always be classified into one of three categories:

1. Overt acts of war such as World War I and World War II.

2. Leader-driven threats where a leader's individual power and charisma creates (or stops) a crisis. There's a very long list of

examples, but think: Kim Jong-un, John F. Kennedy, and Martin Luther King Jr.

3. Terrorism and other far-reaching singular acts such as assassination, hostage taking, and suicide bombers. Examples include the Boston Marathon Bombing and 9/11.

Planned attacks on our economy, our health, and our freedom create stock market disasters because of the intent to harm. With intent comes threat, and with threat comes humankind's natural fight-or-flight response mechanisms. In North Carolina, Taheri-azar claimed he intended retribution for the killing of Muslims overseas. Investors may not have understood what that meant specifically, but they knew that they see trucks driving by every day. Just like buying a lottery ticket and thinking it will be the special one, those investors see the next truck driving by and easily envision it to be the "special" one that is driven by a terrorist.

An instinctual need to protect ourselves arises when we are intentionally threatened by some kind of enemy. The most basic form of natural protection is to gather together and do the same thing at the same time. This "safety in numbers" reaction is almost always *not* the path of a Prepared Investor.

Systemic Crisis

A systemic crisis, on the other hand, involves something that is natural and doesn't intend violence, even if some occurs. It affects the environment uniformly because this type of crisis doesn't willfully target anything. Systemic crises often don't get a serious reaction from investors. This heartening fact stems from the reality that most situations can be interpreted so differently; perception varies and therefore so does reaction and response. The needle only moves if enough people feel the same way at the same time. Our auction-style stock market requires a lot of concerted buying or selling to see a major rise or fall in value. When there's controversy and people disagree about how upsetting something is, then the stock market response isn't so dramatic.

The truly devastating crises, the ones that will meaningfully affect the stock market, require the vast majority of people to act in concert. But most systemic crises just don't unify investors that way. For example, when the gross domestic product (or some other economic indicator) goes up or down, only some will consider that a crisis, others will celebrate it, and the rest will deem it unimportant. The nation's debt could get better like it did during the Clinton years and get worse like it did during the Obama years. Crisis? Opportunity? Insignificant?

People have myriad motivations and perspectives, and some will see a crisis and some won't. Whatever they see, a systemic crisis can almost always be identified as one of three types: market-based, non-market, and irreversible change.

Market-Based Systemic Crisis

Economic and financial systems can fail or otherwise experience major, temporary problems. Market movers like the Saving and Loan Crisis, Black Monday, and the Financial Crisis of 2008 fall into this category. Ironically, Wall Street's one-size-fits-all "just stay the course and do nothing" is actually a one-size-fits-one because when a market-based systemic crisis occurs, this is the moment when the stopped clock is accurate. These occasional breakdowns in society's financial systems are always temporary and notoriously difficult to predict.

When financial advisors talk about risk management and diversification, they usually (whether they know it or not) are talking about preparing for this one type of crisis. You are probably already prepared for this crisis simply because the vast majority of wealth management strategies today are geared to help investors weather a market-based systemic crisis. When a teenager says, "I have a cell phone so I've got every possible vehicular emergency covered," it's the same as an investor saying, "I have a diversified portfolio and so I'm prepared for every type of crisis."

Wall Street treats all crises the same despite the fact that people react to the threat of war very differently from other crises like disease, systemic medical incompetence, or the failure to maintain a country's transportation infrastructure. Market-based systemic crises are the part of the iceberg that's poking out of the ocean. Everyone can see it. For most people, this is the whole story. *The Prepared Investor* focuses on the massive glacier beneath the surface that isn't yet visible to the naked eye.

Non-market Systemic Crisis

Each of the previous examples—the Cincinnati ambulance, the Oklahoma tornado, and the North Carolina trucker—are systemic in nature. The tires degrade whether the driver is in the ambulance or not. The tornado touches down whether people live in Oklahoma or not. Everyone who stays up late experiences fatigue.

A non-market systemic crisis is one without an active enemy so investors do not feel a connection to any reason to sell their investments. Examples include a flood in Mississippi, a train jumping the tracks due to a bridge collapse in Arizona, the mass death of whales in the Pacific Ocean, or millions of animals dying in a tragic Australian forest fire. Humans are hardwired to accept nature, and therefore, when a non-market systemic crisis occurs, investors tend to be more controlled and less panicked (if there's any reaction in the stock market at all).

But there is an exception that creates an opportunity for a Prepared Investor. It's important to be aware of these non-market systemic crises because they can occasionally affect the stock market in a very predictable, and temporary, way. The moment to look for is when that non-market systemic crisis clearly and directly affects some kind of major economic requirement or financial infrastructure. For example, if a serious flood (normally not a market mover) knocked out all the options trading platforms in Chicago, that would be the kind of catalyst that would cause investors to temporarily panic and the market to drop in value. The following case study asks the question, "When does a non-market systemic crisis affect people's portfolios?"

CASE STUDY Hurricane Sandy and COVID-19

"The 2012 superstorm known as Hurricane Sandy wreaked havoc beyond the Eastern Seaboard and reached Northeast Ohio as well, with heavy rain, wind gusts of nearly 70 miles per hour and waves on Lake Erie reaching 15 to 18 feet."
—CONGRESSWOMAN MARCIA LOUISE FUDGE

History has given us many examples of a non-market systemic crisis making the leap from "natural so investors don't care" to "directly causing the stock market to drop." Pandemic diseases, weather, new inventions, and general decay—each a crisis in their own way—all fail to excite fear and panic in the stock market until investors perceive a direct impact on the financial world. For example, Hurricane Ivan struck the United States in September 2004 and caused over $20 billion in damage (including destroying my parents' home in Pensacola, Florida). But the investment markets didn't react meaningfully to the storm. It was a Category 5 hurricane—the worst level that exists—but investors didn't sell stocks because Ivan was a weather system. People understood it as something natural that comes and goes and was separate from the investing world.

Hurricane Sandy, on the other hand, made the leap from unfortunate weather system to immediately affecting investors. Sandy flew right into New York City at the point where the Hudson River meets the Atlantic Ocean and caused serious damage to Wall Street and stock exchange infrastructure. The storm forced the stock market to close for two days in late October 2012, and it didn't reopen until Halloween. If you look up the 2012 S&P 500 index from late October to early December, you'll see a very clear drop and quick rise back to normal. The markets were affected by this weather event as a large number of people sold their investments, causing it to drop very badly, very quickly. This drop-and-rise pattern is something we'll talk about a lot in the chapters ahead because a Prepared Investor can take advantage of it.

The outbreak of the novel coronavirus COVID-19 is another

example of the concept that *investors panic when a non-market systemic crisis directly impacts financial systems or infrastructure*. We will discuss COVID-19 again later in the book, but for now, let's recall the panic and worldwide quarantine that arose from the quick spread of the virus at the beginning of 2020. Many readers already know that the stock market fell, but when specifically did it start to fall and why?

On December 31, 2019, the World Health Organization was notified of the existence of the virus in Wuhan, China. Social media and television kept the world informed throughout January and February as U.S. authorities started screening passengers in major airports for the virus on January 17. Over the next few weeks, vacationers with Holland America and Princess Cruises were stuck for days on cruise ships in quarantine. By mid-February, the virus was in at least twenty-eight countries, and yet a quick look at the S&P 500 index from January 1 through Valentine's Day shows very little reaction from investors. In fact, if you use Google Trends to examine what people were searching for during that time period, you'll see that interest in the virus was waning the first week of February. At that time, people were clearly thinking that the virus was not new or scary nor did they see it directly affecting the economy.

And they were right. The novel coronavirus COVID-19 was neither new nor unknown to investors because SARS had hit in 2002, the H1N1 swine flu hit in 2009, and MERS struck in 2012. But something spooked investors. Something happened to cause the virus to leap from "not very interesting" to "directly affecting the economy," and if you expand your S&P 500 chart so it runs for the entire first quarter 2020, you'll see that happened right around February 23.

China's norms are considered foreign to westerners, and if there is an entire city in the East on lockdown, the rest of the world notices but doesn't get frightened. Westerners think, "They do things their way and we do things our way." But as soon as Italy started to place entire towns under quarantine on February 23, investors noticed and the market began to drop.

It's very easy to understand that if people can't work, financial infrastructure will be badly affected. You didn't have to be a Wall

Street analyst to know that if entire communities aren't working or making money, the economy will suffer. The stock market dropped a lot further a few weeks later when, on March 8 and 9 the entire country of Italy was forcibly quarantined. The pattern in the markets that ensued looks very similar to the one created by Hurricane Sandy, and, later in the book, we'll explore in more detail how to use this pattern to protect and even grow your net worth while the majority of society reacts in fear.

Irreversible Systemic Change

These are major social shifts that, once complete, can never be undone. They are so wide-reaching that nearly everyone is affected and their lives completely changed. Consider the new lines drawn in society as the combustion engine replaced horses. It was the same with the Yellow Pages after the internet came along. At the start, it's a kind of crisis that people resist. But as time goes by, the public attitude changes until, finally, no one would go back to the way it was. Because of this, it's helpful to divide irreversible systemic change into three parts: resistance to the crisis, ambivalence to the change, and finally, acceptance of the benefits.

If investors are on the wrong side of an irreversible systemic change, it can be devastating to their net worth. This kind of crisis can be more sweeping and permanent than any other so it's very important to be able to identify them and adapt your investments in a timely manner. If you don't, you run the risk of being left behind like film-focused Kodak or the movie rental chain Blockbuster.

Ultimately, meaningful systemic change is both beneficial to society and often incredibly slow. The positive aspect explains why the transition occurs, and the slow aspect means it's difficult to find an immediate, dramatic impact in the stock market. That's why meaningful, irreversible change doesn't typically result in the same stock market patterns as other crises. By examining the current public climate for a given topic, a Prepared Investor can gauge how far along society is in regard to the change. For example, while traveling by horseback is out because cars are fully accepted, completely automated restaurants are still something society resists.

These irreversible systemic changes start out as a crisis, but then, over time, people become ambivalent until finally there's acceptance. Even though the change is usually for the better, humans typically resist the "crisis" until it's the new normal and then they wouldn't want to go back to the old way at all. Changing the conversation about preparing financially for crisis means accepting that an irreversible systemic change is different from a hurricane or a virus. What's more, a Prepared Investor can take advantage of systemic trends, which is why the next chapter focuses on recognizing irreversible systemic change and the opportunities that come with it.

CHAPTER TWO

Irreversible Systemic Change
What It Looks Like and
How to Prepare

Wall Street acts like everything bad that happens in the invest-ment world is a market-based systemic crisis. But we now know that this isn't the case. There is an abundance of systemic crises that are natural and don't intend or plan violence and rarely move the markets meaningfully in the short term. But in the case of one type of systemic crisis—irreversible systemic change—your financial independence may be truly lost if you fail to recognize the situation and adapt accordingly. To someone who is unprepared, this type of systemic crisis can be the most devastating of all. Not only can you lose money, but if you cling to the obsolete, your quality of life suffers as well.

> **ACTION STEP #2: Know how to identify irreversible systemic change even if, in the short term, the stock market does not.**

Many irreversible systemic changes appear to have a compelling argument on both sides of the issue, making it extremely difficult to know if it warrants action. For example, is climate change really the world-altering crisis that so many people both deny and believe in? Is obesity, sugary sodas, or sitting down too much the next major systemic crisis? You could spend years studying all the facts from both sides. Whether your concern is climate change, refined sugar, or the loss of the rain forest, it's important not to allow your passion for a certain cause to misalign your investment portfolio.

Take, for example, some work my firm did in 2014 for a client who was worried about the irreversible systemic change surrounding colony collapse disorder (CCD) and the loss of honeybees. At the time, this issue was already more than a decade old and the controversy was terribly convoluted. For some people, the bees were dying and it meant a complete loss of certain pollinated foods as well as a major blow to the nation's food supply capabilities. For others, the bees were dying, but it wasn't really going to be a problem at all. Still others questioned if the bees were really dying at rates worthy of alarm. There was some debate over whether CCD could be fixed by using less insecticides versus the idea that perhaps it was just a normal, temporary phenomenon needing no attention at all.

With a fierce desire to champion the bees' cause, my client saw a connection between the honeybees dying and the loss of pollinated fruits and vegetables. In this direct "cause and effect" scenario, he expected that, due to the supply of those foods declining, the cost of fruits and vegetables would increase as demand stayed the same. In his zeal for proving his opinion was the right one, he wanted to revise his portfolio holdings to capitalize on the increased cost of fruits and vegetables. With hindsight we know this was a mistake as there's been no major food shortage due to CCD. How can we keep our passion for tomorrow's controversy from affecting our overall financial independence?

From an investor's point of view, there are three questions, which I refer to as Meaningful Change Questions, that make it easy to cut through the noise and focus on the few long-term systemic changes worthy of action.

1. Does this change make an important part of society easier, cheaper, or faster?

2. Does this change provide people more freedom, more authority, or more individual capability?

3. Did you answer "no" to both questions 1 and 2? If so, consider taking action only if the sole voice against change comes from those who benefit if things stay the same.

If you answer "no" to the first two questions and there are different views on the issue, you'll probably want to stay away from retooling your portfolio around that concern until there's more empirical evidence. Using the bees as an example, the answer to the first question is that CCD does not make society better. Nor does the loss of honeybees provide us more freedom. Lastly, there were many different views on what was happening with the bees and, as we discussed in the last chapter, it's tough to meaningfully move the stock market when there's not a majority in agreement. Using these three questions as a gauge will allow you to avoid the highly controversial, hotly debated topics that have good points on both sides and, usually, are emotionally charged. The goal in asking these questions is not to become prophets who can predict the future of global warming or argue whether or not electric vehicles will completely replace all cars on the road. Rather, these three questions will help to heighten your ability to protect and grow your portfolio by identifying irreversible systemic change faster than others.

Often considered a crisis at its infancy, systemic change of an irreversible nature slowly catches on until finally there's widespread acceptance. Back in the 1930s, for example, the medical establishment was against the use of antibiotics, which definitely improved an important part of society: our health. It wasn't long before antibiotics completely changed the hospital experience and no one today would want to use outdated medical methods. It's the same for the handwritten letter versus an email. While doing public speaking, I'll sometimes ask retired audience members if they remember their initial reaction to email back when it first was available. The vast majority of them didn't like it in the beginning even though they almost all use it regularly today. After all the time and experimentation to reach the point that a person can simply turn a knob and get a stove burner lit, humans aren't going to keep gathering wood and blowing on sparks to light a fire. Antibiotics, email, and gas heat made parts of society easier, cheaper, or faster (question 1) and provided people more freedom, more authority, or more individual capability (question 2).

Irreversible systemic change is an important kind of crisis for the Prepared Investor because of the dramatic disadvantages that come from ignoring the trends. The following case studies identify three current irreversible systemic changes and highlight how to use the Meaningful Change Questions on your own.

CASE STUDY Women's Rights

Against the backdrop of the 1960s, the female half of the U.S. population began to seize their own piece of the American dream. Women of all backgrounds were championed and became champions for themselves in ways never before seen. At the time of the Equal Rights Amendment, Americans and their political leaders considered equality among sexes a highly charged and deeply controversial crisis. Allow women to go to college? That would shrink their reproductive organs. Employ women in paying jobs outside the home? That would destroy families. Exercise their right to vote in national elections? Why should they bother themselves with such matters? Participate in sports? No proper lady would ever want to perspire. There was clearly much resistance to the "crisis" of equality.

These issues were unthinkably scandalous because it was a time when a bank could refuse to issue a credit card to an unmarried woman; and if she was married, her husband was required to co-sign. Women could not serve on a jury because they were considered the center of the home. In the 1960s, open discussions on reproductive freedom and a woman's right to decide whether and when to have children were just beginning. It wasn't until 1969 that a woman could gain admittance to an Ivy League education at Yale or Princeton while Harvard's regular undergraduate bachelor's degree remained all-male until 1972.

Scholars credit the origin of the women's rights movement to Esther Peterson, who was director of the Women's Bureau of the U.S. Department of Labor in 1961. She considered it to be the government's responsibility to take an active role in addressing discrimination against women. Not long after, in 1963, Betty Freidan published her book *The Feminine Mystique*, which evolved out of a survey she conducted for her twenty-year college reunion. In it, she documented how limited options in life oppressed middle-class educated women emotionally and intellectually. The book became an immediate bestseller and inspired thousands of women to look for fulfillment beyond the role of homemaker.

Title VII of the Civil Rights Act of 1964 prohibited employment discrimination on the basis of gender, as well as race, religion, and national origin. Some say the category of gender was included in the bill as a last-ditch effort to ensure it would not pass. But it did pass, and the Equal Employment Opportunity Commission was established to investigate discrimination complaints. In its first five years, the commission received almost 50,000 sex discrimination complaints.

Had you used the Meaningful Change Questions back in the late 1960s, there would have been a resounding "yes!" to the second question, "Does this change provide people more freedom, more authority, or more individual capability?" Even now, the movement continues as #MeToo, reminding us that much of society still struggles to reach the even playing field imagined by Esther Peterson and Bettie Freidan.

Readers today might not appreciate the depth of change and the social crisis the country had to navigate to get to this point. But consider this: if you'd owned a bank back in the 1960s, you woke up one day to suddenly learn that you had double the customers from the day before. Today, there are entire industries built around women as consumers, leaders, and influencers. A Prepared Investor who had identified this trend back when it was a crisis could have guided their investing efforts with questions like:

- "Which companies are embracing this cultural shift better than others?"

- "How well are companies adapting to the changing demand?"

- "What products work better after this change or now exist because of it?"

CASE STUDY **The Impending Fall of Diamonds**

It is the norm today to buy a diamond ring as part of a marriage proposal. Have Americans always needed a diamond to help profess their love? Investigative journalist Edward Jay Epstein asked that question back in 1982 when he wrote the article "Have You Ever Tried to Sell a Diamond?" In this article, he positioned the "diamond invention" as the "creation of the idea that diamonds are rare and valuable, and are essential signs of esteem." He goes on to explain that the rise of the diamond began when British businessmen launched a South Africa–based monopoly, De Beers Consolidated Mines, Ltd., to control all facets of the diamond trade as a result of the flood of so-called rare diamonds in the late 1800s.

Controlling the supply was the first half of the effort to prop up diamonds as the store of value that De Beers claimed. In 1938, Harry Oppenheimer, the De Beers founder's son, recruited the New York–based ad agency, N. W. Ayer & Son, to help with the second half of that effort: control the demand side of the diamond jewelry business by persuading society that only diamonds could convey a young man's commitment, his offer of romance, his love, even his personal and professional success. The larger the diamond, Ayer suggested, the more that young woman should be impressed. Conversely, Ayer provided warnings to the suitors who failed to conclude a courtship with the purchase of a diamond. About ten years later, an Ayer copywriter created a slogan that every reader of this book will immediately recognize: "A Diamond Is Forever." By 1979, the De Beers portion of the wholesale diamond trade in the United States had increased from $23 million to $2.1 billion.

In the 2018 *New York Times* article "A Battle Over Diamonds: Made by Nature or in Lab," Jeffrey D. Feero, managing partner of Alex Sepkus, a high-end jewelry designer, said, "I don't consider most diamonds rare and unusual. Diamonds are a commodity with tightly controlled sourcing and marketing." Alan Bronstein, president of the Natural Color Diamond Association and a diamond trader himself, was also quoted saying, "Maybe two, three, four percent of diamonds have the opportunity to appreciate over time."

The fact that diamonds are not rare should be enough to make a Prepared Investor raise an eyebrow. But add to that fact the developing technology that allows people to create real diamonds in a lab, and diamonds' high prices cannot last. Back in the 1950s, the first man-made diamonds were used by General Electric for industrial purposes. By the 1980s, the technology had advanced enough that the diamonds could be used as jewelry. Today, they are virtually indistinguishable from their counterparts, which are mined from the earth.

In the same article about synthetic jewelry, the *New York Times* cited a famous diamond retailer advertising, "We know that when it comes to finding your perfect diamond, you want options. In that spirit we present our exclusive Lab-Grown E3 Diamond. The E3 diamond is identical in every way to a diamond mined from the Earth. It exhibits the same exceptional color, clarity, beauty, and brilliance as a mined diamond because it is identical in composition to a mined diamond. Yes, identical. Not a simulation. Not a fake. We're talking molecular level stuff. It's a diamond—evolved. E3, a beautiful choice to consider as the centerpiece of your engagement ring." Another retailer was cited saying, "Think of this as making ice in your freezer versus getting it from a glacier; both are ice regardless of the origin."

It's not just those in the business of selling man-made diamonds that say they are the same as their mined counterparts. The Gemological Institute of America (GIA) defines the material "diamond" as carbon atoms in a cubic structure. Both natural and man-made diamonds are made of this material. The GIA warns that even a skilled jeweler or trained gemologist cannot distinguish them without extremely specialized equipment. This was convincingly demonstrated by the CNBC Make It team in New York City's famous diamond district. It was reported in June 2019 that the man-made diamond engagement ring CNBC offered for sale fooled many experienced jewelers into offering far too much money for what they thought was a natural diamond.

Brenda Harwick, manager of on-campus and lab gemology instruction for GIA offers insight in Amanda Luke's article on the GIA website saying, "One of the beautiful aspects of a polished dia-mond is the way light interacts with it, and it has superior hardness on the Mohs scale. A synthetic diamond has those properties as well." Cape Town Diamond Museum reported in 2016, "Scientists believe a lab-grown diamond still counts as a real diamond; the physical properties and chemical composition of a synthetic diamond are the same as a natural diamond." GQ writer Stephanie Talmadge wrote in October 2018, "Lab-grown diamonds lack inclusions . . . making them appear more brilliant [than a diamond mined from the earth]."

This movement away from mined diamonds is still not complete today, and at the time of this writing, most people are somewhat aware of these facts, but they don't care enough to change their diamond-buying behavior. While society is still ambivalent to this irreversible systemic change, a Prepared Investor would seriously consider selling the diamonds they currently own before the prices change too much. Also, it should be much harder now for the dia-mond industry to convince you to buy another pretty rock mined from the earth.

Using the Meaningful Change Questions, we can answer "yes" to the question, "Does this change clearly make an important part of society easier, cheaper, or faster?" Attractive jewelry is getting more accessible and less expensive. It happens that the third question sup-ports this too because, up until the late 1990s, De Beers was the only voice saying there's no substitute for natural diamonds.

In the next and final part of this case study, we'll dive into an extremely pervasive systemic change that feels to many like a crisis because it is in its infancy right now. For many people, the fact that robots will be better workers than humans represents a very serious and frightening crisis. Artificial intelligence is just as inevitable as the decline of the Yellow Pages after the dawn of the internet and will affect every American in some way.

CASE STUDY The Rise of Artificial Intelligence

When clients come into my office, they usually ask about the headlines. Their questions about Russia, China, and North Korea are a big reason why I wrote this book. No one has ever come into my office and asked, "How will changing women's rights or the decline of diamonds affect my portfolio?" Systemic changes move slowly so we don't typically worry about them in front of the more threatening ones like a terrorist attack. Yet they can be much more dramatically influential over the long term. We have only to look at the game of chess and the Olympics for excellent examples of this.

The world of chess has already experienced an irreversible, system-destroying change that began back in May 1997. That's when IBM's Deep Blue computer defeated Garry Kasparov, the world's chess champion at the time. This created a social shock because people back then believed a computer could never beat a person. The prevailing idea was that a human's creativity would always outsmart a computer's computational ability. Following Kasparov's defeat, a period of human-robot collaboration dominated chess. For about fourteen years, a computer paired with a human player was an unbeatable combination in elite chess competitions, until finally the human partner was holding the computer back. Right around the time that IBM's Watson competed alone against two human contestants and won the game show *Jeopardy*, the steady march toward an ineffective human chess player had concluded.

Starting in 2011, computers battled each other at the highest levels of chess play, and by 2016, it was clear that the world chess champion was a computer program named StockFish 8. This program was unassailably the best chess player in existence until December 2017, when Google asked for an informal matchup between their artificial intelligence and StockFish 8. It was a David-vs-Goliath match, and no one expected Google's AI to win. StockFish 8 was Goliath with hundreds of years of experience at its cyber fingertips. Google's AI, called Alpha Zero, wasn't even given the rules of the game until the day of the match. This meant that Alpha Zero had only four hours of chess experience and less than one-tenth of the computational capability of StockFish 8. To put that in perspective, Google's AI could look at eight chess positions in the same time that StockFish 8 could look at 7,000. Naturally, the world expected Alpha Zero to lose.

Normally, when two programs play chess, they'll play a series of one hundred games. If the contestants are evenly matched, one program will win two or three games and the other program will win two or three as well. The rest of the one hundred games are ties. Knowing this helps drive home the enormity of Alpha Zero winning *twenty-eight times* while the reigning champion never won once.

Some of the winning moves were so unusual, it's appropriate to say they were creative. Chess masters who have reviewed those games say they see techniques and strategies they've never even imagined. This particular artificial intelligence went from inexperience and unawareness to complete domination in only a few hours. In all-human chess matches today, chess judges are constantly on the lookout for computer-aided cheating. And how do they find it? When a person's move is spectacularly creative, that's the sign that it cannot be a human's move. The very thing that, twenty years earlier, was deemed impossible for machines to do—creative moves—is now the red flag used to keep the humans honest.

Students of the philosopher and author Yuval Noah Harari will have recognized some of this chess story from his book *21 Lessons for the 21st Century*. However, since there's an argument that this AI is only effective in closed systems (like a chessboard with a limited number of possibilities), let's examine another scenario brought to my attention by Louise Radnofsky, an Oxford and Colombia grad who has reported for the *Wall Street Journal* for over a decade.

When gymnasts do their flips and leaps, a panel of judges scores them as best as their human eyes can see. But even at the highest levels of competition, bias is accepted as a fact of the game. It's impossible to avoid human subjectivity, and competitors at the global level understand that judges will give more or less emphasis to certain movements of their body.

In May 2017, the company Fujitsu created an AI that they claimed could judge gymnastic competitions. Just like in chess, the initial response was one of great disbelief that a program would be able to judge a gymnast's routine and the artistry involved. It's still a popular idea today that people's creativity sets them apart from machines. Nevertheless, about two years after its announcement, Fujitsu's AI was approved for use on a trial basis by the International Gymnastics Federation.

In March 2019, the AI was used in Stuttgart, Germany, to help judge a small portion of the Individual All-Around World Cup. The experiment was such a resounding success that this AI was contractually obligated to judge one-half of all gymnastics events in the Tokyo 2020 Olympics (which incidentally were postponed at the time of this writing). It is also already contractually committed to judge *all* the gymnastics events in the Paris 2024 Olympics. Even gymnastics legend Valorie Kondos Field, who retired as an icon for the number of championships she helped UCLA win in row, has announced that she thinks robots will do an amazing job judging gymnasts' routines.

There will never be another human chess champion. There's a clear time table for how long it will be until the human gymnastics judge is irrelevant as well. If this pattern continues, we have an irreversible systemic change worthy of a Prepared Investor's attention. It's a crisis right now because humankind is losing its effectiveness. The human became dead weight in the game of chess, and the Olympics judge is sure to go the same way. Why not also in the game of productivity and occupation? Aren't our jobs at risk?

I'm not suggesting that nobody will have a job in the future. Rather, I'm pointing out that this change is different from previous ones. In the past, a cavalryman could learn new skills and become a tank driver. But this isn't that kind of change. This is more like the cavalryman's horse being put out to pasture because tanks and jeeps have engines to move them. Does anyone think that, as technology advances, humans themselves will be driving tanks? Will we even be driving our regular cars at home?

The Massachusetts Institute of Technology offers its own insights in the *MIT Work of the Future Report*. Put together by a group of scientists and academics led by L. Rafael Reif, the university's president, the report is the culmination of almost two years of their investigation into how emerging technologies will impact employment. It's important to remember that they are not an impartial group. They love technology and robots, and they want other people to love them as well. That's why their report says in various ways that there's nothing to worry about because robots are not going to take over the world.

But it's very telling that the report also describes how the middle class is going to get smaller and smaller as almost all the jobs performed by this part of the population can be done by a robot. However, the scientists and academics making this prediction propose that the job losses ahead are not technology's fault. Instead, they claim it is the inevitable result of a capitalistic society. They suggest the robots are not to blame and instead point the finger at America's love of "the corporate shareholder that results in policies that encourage capital investments instead of investments in labor." It appears that, whether you are an academic at MIT (like them) or a business owner in Texas (like me), we agree there's going to be a lot less jobs.

I've been a member of Mensa for many years, and a fellow Mensan named Nikhil Cheerla suggests there's more to this story. With Stanford University roots, Cheerla teaches AI programming online, and he suggests that software like Alpha Zero is less a programming accomplishment and much more about the hardware. Alpha Zero learned chess by playing itself for a few hours on Google's most advanced hardware called tensor processing units. These are conceivably thousands of times faster than any hardware available just a few years ago. In a very real sense, Alpha Zero couldn't have existed until now because the processing technology simply wasn't there. If it's about the hardware, then this begs the question, "What's to come?"

To give you an idea of what to expect, in May 2019 various journals reported that two scientists at MIT discovered a way to make a neural network 90 percent smaller. This is the hardware that gives AI its intelligence, and they were able to get the same smarts in a tenth of the size. Most of the time, we hear about technology doubling its capacity or halving in size. A *90 percent* reduction is astonishing.

The growing abilities of AI are already affecting lawmakers as well. Recently, Microsoft President Brad Smith called for the U.S. government to consider requiring human oversight of facial-recognition technologies. America is probably a bit behind the European Union on this. They've already enacted the General Data Protection Regulation, which establishes the right for individuals to know about and to challenge automated decisions. RAND, a nonprofit global research firm, has formally suggested that the United States needs processes that would allow people to appeal machine-made decisions. A critical part of their suggestion is that those appeals must be heard by other humans.

Tomorrow is here. If you agree with Yuval Noah Harari, L. Rafael Reif, and Nikhil Cheerla, it's wise to expect a large part of society will be unable to offer meaningful value and therefore cannot receive meaningful pay. While this change sounds very frightening, it's important to remember it will happen slowly, which means you can prepare for this. The next two action steps directly address the rise of artificial intelligence and are also foundational ideas that all Prepared Investors should seriously consider. By just doing these steps and nothing else, you'll be so much further along on your journey to being prepared for crisis.

ACTION STEP #3: Save everything first. Then, schedule your designated monthly spending.

The idea that you must save for your future isn't new, and the advantages of having extra money every month are obvious. What is not as clear is how to accomplish this, especially in the face of materialism and a strong culture of "keeping up with the Joneses." What if there was an easy way to control your lifestyle and make sure you saved every month?

Most Americans go to work and get their pay into their checking account. Some of what they earn is already removed from their paycheck to cover taxes, insurance, and perhaps retirement savings. The funds that are left get deposited in their checking account, and that's where they pull from to pay their bills. If they spend all this money, that is called living paycheck to paycheck, which is much more common than you think. Nevertheless, there are people who make difficult choices, lower their bills, and are able to save.

The vast majority of these savers designate a fixed amount to save each month. Some people will say, "Out of sight, out of mind," and have the fixed amount of savings removed automatically from their checking account every month so they are sure to save on a regular basis. This is called designated saving because the same amount goes into savings each month.

While that is better than no savings at all, this typical setup has a serious flaw in the long term. As the years go by and people get their pay raises or the occasional bonus, there is more and more money coming into the checking account at different times. What happens to that "extra" money? They spend it because people think, "I've already saved my consistent amount each month." This phenomenon is called lifestyle creep, and it destroys the ability to grow net worth over time.

Lifestyle creep occurs because all the extra money you earn from garage sales, future promotions, overtime, bonuses, and side jobs is available to spend as it gets deposited into the operational checking account. There is another way. Imagine for a moment that we switch the initial account, your typical checking account, where you receive your pay. So now, you get all your pay into your savings account. Each month, your savings account receives all the money—everything—you and your family make instead of its going to checking. Then, you designate a fixed amount that goes to your checking account on a regular basis. This means that, as you get pay raises over time, the extra money is not available for spending. It's already been saved.

A dual-income couple shared with me that they knew they had more than enough money coming in and were saving every month, but they were frustrated that their savings account didn't seem to change much. She was a consultant for a Fortune 500 company, and he was a lender working with a major U.S. bank. Going back over their finances, we could easily see that their regular salaries were not "regular" at all. In the previous five years, they'd earned three promotions and seven bonuses, and she had a couple periods of major overtime related to a consulting project. During the entire five years, they saved the same amount of money each month, and, what's worse, we realized it was a savings figure they'd selected back at the start of their marriage when finances were a lot different.

Imagine how those five years could have changed their net worth if they had fixed their lifestyle and saved the extra instead of fixing their savings and growing their lifestyle. When all pay goes directly to savings, your monthly budget of what you spend won't change unless you purposefully go in and change that fixed amount coming into your checking account. This is a powerful, lifelong method to ensure that you truly control your finances and grow your net worth. It changes the question from, "How can I save?" to "How do I use my savings wisely?"

ACTION STEP #4: Don't use your savings to buy things that cost money. Instead, buy things that make money.

Now that you are systemically controlling your lifestyle and saving all extras, the next step is to use those funds in a way that truly will protect your future. The only rule to follow is to buy things that make you more money or accomplish some meaningful requirement in your life. When you buy a bigger house, another luxury car, or a fancy boat, you are showing people that you *used to have money*.

There are a lot of ways to buy things that create more money, but if we're talking about being prepared for the irreversible systemic change unfolding from the advancements in artificial intelligence and robotics, then there's probably only one purchase that makes sense. Use the extra money to buy and hold publicly traded companies. Company ownership—as in buying and holding stocks—means you will reap the benefits that all these machines are working toward. When a company fires its people and replaces them with machines, as a part owner of that business, you will benefit. As those machines work and get better at being productive and useful, you will reap the financial rewards of their efforts.

In the agricultural societies of the past—the days of serfs and lords of the manor—land determined nobility. Land and real estate were the currency that provided security and stability. Soon that land will be intelligent machines, and the question will be, "Who owns the most robots?" AI and the hardware empowered by it aren't citizens. Both are considered property. Robots will be owned by companies and governments (and to a lesser extent individuals). The best way to own a piece of the new "land" of the future is to own the companies that use and make robots. While they are still inexpensive and people continue to grapple with how AI is changing our world, let these questions guide your efforts:

- "Which companies are embracing this technological shift better than others?"

- "How well are companies adapting to the changing technologies?"

- "What AI products work better or now exist because of these changes?"

The Power of Perception: Threats and the Stock Market

In all systemic crises, whether it's robots, bees, or the technology bubble, perception trumps reality. People react to what they think is occurring, which isn't necessarily the same thing as what's truly happening. For example, in the summer of 2019, a serious heat wave

turned deadly in the United States in a much-lamented natural phenomenon. In keeping with what we've learned about non-market
systemic crisis, no one worried that the sun was out to get them.
Society mourned the heat-wave tragedy without feeling the fear of
an active, intentional threat and therefore wasn't pressed to change
any investments.

Now, let's change the heat-wave example by pretending that
society was convinced, whether right or wrong, that the heat wave
was the result of a new weapon being used by Vladimir Putin. It's
the exact same temperature each day and the exact same results, but
in this imaginary scenario, there would be a much different public
reaction. Investors' panic and fear arise not from the disaster itself
but from the intent to harm. That panic, whether or not this hypothetical heat-wave weapon exists, creates pressure to act, and the
stock market would fall as a result. Therefore, the greatest crises in
history, and in the future, are threatening in nature. We turn now to
our first of three categories of threatening crisis: the overt act of war.

CHAPTER THREE

Overt Acts of War

How Investors Can Prepare for the Next "Big One"

To be fully prepared to change a flat tire, you must be able to recognize that moment when a car tire is dangerously low on air. In the same way, to be a Prepared Investor, it's critical that you can identify when a specific catalyst, such as an overt act of war, marks the beginning of a crisis. While there are multiple categories of threatening crises, we begin with overt acts of war because the starting moment is so obvious. An overt act of war, by definition, leaves nothing to the imagination. There's no debate about the existence of conflict, even if there's controversy surrounding its legitimacy. It's the equivalent of walking out to your car in the parking lot and immediately seeing that the tire is flat.

Far less subtle than any systemic crisis, an overt act of war is a dramatic, state-level conflict or the action that immediately precedes conflict. It is the spark, the catalyst, that makes the fire of war, as well as the investor response, inevitable. As the first of three types of threatening crises, it is also the rarest in modern day. When the next one occurs, however, whether it is a surprise attack by one country against another or a formal declaration of war, it will be the next "big one." A Prepared Investor will be ready to take appropriate action to protect, and even grow, their portfolio because, with a quick examination of history, it's easy to understand the basic patterns to expect.

From America's point of view, it was an overt act of war that marked the country's entry into both World War I and World War

II. In both scenarios, the conflict raged outside the United States long before America itself got involved. For World War II, the crisis hit the United States when Japan attacked Pearl Harbor, transforming a war between European and Asian countries into a problem for America as well. The United States entered World War I much less dramatically with a formal declaration of war by the United States Congress.

Prior to entering World War I, America remained both aloof and neutral while powers abroad engaged in conflict. In the two years before the United States declared war in 1917, it was unclear whether Americans were sympathetic to the Central Powers led by Germany or to the Allied Powers led by Britain. Both of those countries made efforts to sway the U.S. to their side. Much like Russians using Facebook today to influence Americans, Germany took out advertisements in U.S. newspapers warning of ocean travel where the Germans might need to defend themselves against British military efforts. One of those German ads in *The New York Times* cautioned Americans not to book passage on the *Lusitania*, a famous British luxury passenger ship preparing for a transatlantic voyage.

Ultimately, the Germans sank the British passenger liner, and Winston Churchill, Britain's Minister of Munitions, immediately started a powerful publicity campaign to make sure the world was aware of the details behind the sinking of the *Lusitania*. To influence Americans, Churchill helped fan the flames of many inaccurate rumors, such as the idea that Germany had created a "Lusitania medal" honoring their soldiers who had killed civilians. Churchill's propaganda, a precursor to "fake news" today, served its purpose as it helped sway Americans to favor the British side. When the United States did finally enter into World War I after discovering the Germans were trying to incite Mexico to attack America, it joined the Allied Powers with a formal declaration on Good Friday, April 6, 1917.

With this straightforward announcement, America was immediately affected and the general population began to make ready in individual ways. One of the ways to see how Americans reacted to that declaration of war is to examine how the stock market behaved in the days that followed. In the pages ahead, we'll look specifically at the stock market movement immediately following the threatening catalyst for both World War I and World War II to demonstrate that *a pattern exists.*

ACTION STEP #5: Recognize the Act of War Market Pattern.

There is a part of human nature that helps people blend in and hide in plain sight called herd mentality. By going with the herd, individuals don't attract too much attention and lessen the odds they will be singled out by a predator. A CBS News report, "Fear Factor: How Herd Mentality Drives Us," interviewed several experts on this phenomenon. Pat Thomas, a general curator at the Bronx Zoo, told CBS News that if animals "act too much out of the norm, more often than not [they] don't survive very long." Mother Nature convincingly suggests that those who stay scared and run with the herd are more likely to stay alive.

"We are mammals, just like the wildebeest in the plains of the African Savannah," added Andrew Lo, who studies emotions and economics at MIT. Lo's work has led him to believe that, when fear overtakes people, they are compelled to behave like animals, using a part of the brain some scientists call the "mammalian brain." Dr. Gregory Berns experiments with how the brain reacts to fear at Emory University in Georgia. "Whether it's the fear of being the odd person out, whether it's the fear of uncertainty or the fear of losing your shirt in the market, the fear starts to compel you to do something, because a million years ago, that fear meant you probably had to run or fight," Berns said.

But reactions that prepared our ancestors for man-eating saber-toothed tigers don't make as much sense in our modern world of stock exchanges and YouTube videos. Today, it seems laughable that one in ten people in the United States was worried the world would end at the conclusion of the 5,125-year Mayan Calendar on December 21, 2012. *National Geographic* reported, a year beforehand, that experts on the Mesoamerican culture claimed, "It's remotely possible the world will end in December 2012." It was meant as a laughable idea, but by the time December 2012 had arrived, nearly the entire civilized world was paying serious attention. Two days before the supposed end of the world, BBC news reported: "Russians have been so worried that the Minister of Emergency Situations issued a denial that the world would end. Authorities in . . . the South of France have barred access to a mountain where some believe a UFO will rescue them. And survivalists in America . . . have been busy preparing for all manner of cataclysm."

Just days before December 21, 2012, *Scientific American* reported on the connection between a major crisis, such as an overt act of war or a doomsday prophecy, and people's fascination with the postapocalyptic landscape. In the article, Steven Schlozman uses his Harvard Medical School experience and writing accomplishments—his first novel details a zombie apocalypse—to explain why people are drawn to act irrationally in the face of major threat scenarios. Schlozman has found that his therapy patients frequently romanticize the end of times because it's a fantasy world where they have the ability to focus on a threat and not worry about the myriad issues and challenges of everyday life. In fact, Schlozman recently experienced an echo of the "War of the Worlds" broadcast from 1938, when his own radio program was cut short because listeners were taking his fictional book as fact. After a crisis, "all of this uncertainty and all of this fear comes together and people think maybe life would be better," Schlozman says.

Daniel Gilbert, a Harvard psychologist famous for his TED Talks about happiness, was hired by the Department of Homeland Security because he had a radical idea about the war on terror. He suggested that the American security budget related to terrorism would be better spent on ways to educate people and change the country's view of what constitutes a crisis worthy of terror. When someone blows up a bus and thirty people die, is the feeling of terror the proper, rational response? Is that really a crisis? Gilbert says our human nature requires us to respond to an attack, but humankind isn't hardwired to feel horrified by the weather, accidents, or systemic flaws. "If Australia disappears tomorrow, terror is probably the right response," he says.

If someone shoots ten people in a mall, the national reaction shouldn't be worse than the reaction to the more than 3,000 deaths every month on U.S. highways. If a human agent is trying to kill someone, people automatically see the active threat and the possibility of it affecting them. On the other hand, a tree falling on someone or a child drowning in a backyard pool doesn't elicit anywhere near the same response. Systemically, Gilbert explains, poverty is one of the greatest killers of all time and yet, "it's not making headlines . . . it's not flashy."

Humans react to a crisis in a certain way, and they will keep doing it. People are predictably irrational in the face of a threat, which is why training and education are such important parts of preparing for any threatening situation. This predictable, irrational reaction can be seen and described by examining the stock market after an overt act of war. You'll continue to see three basic tenets in the chapters ahead as they define the Act of War Market Pattern.

1. Very quickly after the crisis catalyst, the stock market drops as a result of people selling their investments. All that investors care about at the start of the crisis is the perceived collective threat, whether real or imagined. Rational data doesn't matter.

2. Following the market's decline, there is a trading day when the majority of the companies in the Dow Jones Industrial Average and the S&P 500 rise. The market might not get back to pre-crisis levels here, but this "all up" day is part of the pattern.

3. In less than six months, the market rises to pre-crisis levels. Perhaps it does not exactly surpass the pre-crisis watermark, but it gets close enough to create a clear end to the pattern with the market trading quite a bit higher than the low achieved immediately following the start of the crisis. Overall, the pattern looks similar to a messy letter U, and the vast majority of the time, it all happens in less than sixty days.

On April 5, 1917, the Dow Jones Industrial Average (DJIA) closed at 94.61. The following day, the United States officially entered World War I. In the following chart (figure 3.1), *every single DJIA company dropped* on the first day of trading following the declaration. Not long after, there's a single trading day when almost *every single company rises*. People react with sell orders, and then, just a short while later, they do the exact opposite.

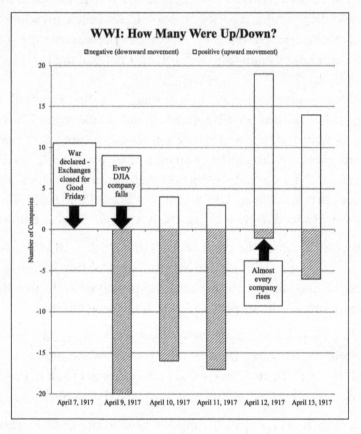

Figure 3.1

This chart shows, graphically, the group reaction of investors to the overt act of war. Companies going up each day are displayed above the chart's midline while the shaded bars below the midline denote the number of companies that dropped in value. It is like watching someone flinch and blink because of a loud noise. It's a natural reaction to the perceived threat created by America's entrance into the Great War. Although the companies people traded on the stock exchanges weren't suddenly going to have zero customers as a result of the war, people immediately flinched and closed their eyes for a quick moment. Mere days later, people reinvested in concert to create an "all-up" day.

On December 7, 1941, eighteen years before Alaska and Hawaii joined America, Japan attacked Pearl Harbor. At this time, the Axis powers led by Germany and Japan were aligned against the Allied Powers led by Britain and the Soviet Union. Just like in World War I, America remained aloof and wasn't taking sides until the surprise attack, which killed more than 2,400 people. To the United States, being directly attacked was an overt act of war and a resounding crisis dubbed "a day that will live in infamy" by President Franklin D. Roosevelt.

The stock market agreed and behaved accordingly as the following chart (figure 3.2 on the next page) demonstrates. In response to this overt act of war, almost every DJIA stock fell. Just like when Congress declared war in World War I, there's a day when almost every single company in the index drops, and then, shortly after, there's a day when they almost all rise again. Investors' opinion about the stock market changed fast as purchases quickly buoyed the index in a measurable display of the natural human reaction to threatening crisis.

The next two charts (figure 3.3 and figure 3.4) show another view of the pattern from start to finish for both World War I and World War II. The panicked drop and then quick decisive rise in 1917 look eerily similar to the reaction in 1941. For a short while, investors were unknowingly acting in concert to complete the U-shaped Act of War Market Pattern before individual motivations and points of view took over again. For a Prepared Investor, recognizing, even anticipating this pattern in response to threatening crises such as an overt act of war, is an excellent step toward being financially prepared to protect and grow your portfolio in the face of the next crisis.

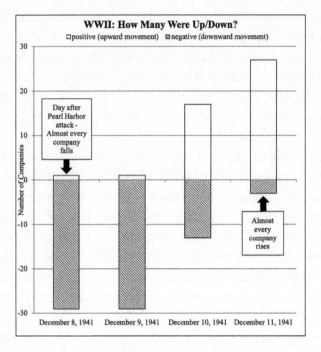

Figure 3.2 (above); Figure 3.3 (below)

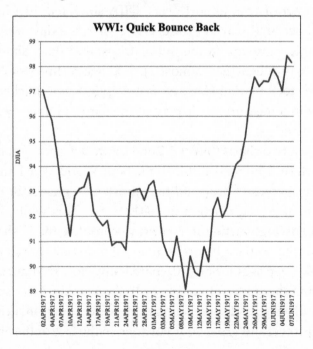

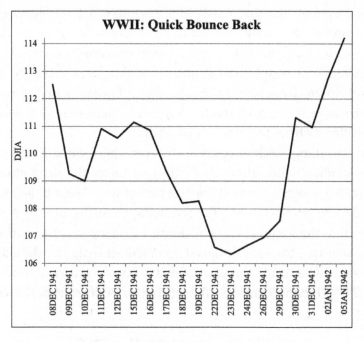

Figure 3.4

The Act of War Market Pattern: Cause and Effect

If the market goes down in response to an overt act of war or some other crisis, this means that more people are selling investments than buying them. Or, more accurately, there are more sales than purchases. This is what causes the investments to change in value. When it comes to the decision to sell, a panicked person might want to sell all their stocks in a company because they fear losing all of their money. For those on a fixed income or otherwise constrained financially, this fear can be particularly acute. In the rare case where an investor might actually pause before reacting, he is much more likely to bury his head in the sand and do nothing rather than ask, "Is it wise or rational to broadly sell investments because the country is going to war? Is it possible that the company I own might be entering a time of increased movement of goods, more traveling, and more production due to our participation in the war?"

A Prepared Investor, on the other hand, is actively looking for opportunities that arise because of an understanding of the Act of War Market Pattern. Part of being ready for crisis is accepting that the majority of people will panic, sell rashly, and drive the stock market down. By accepting this reality, a Prepared Investor finds it easier to separate from the herd and take steps that look and feel very different from the majority of others.

In speaking with investors all over the United States, I've encountered the question, "How do you know the drop after the crisis catalyst was a result of the overt act of war? What if the market was already going down?" The following chart (figure 3.5) demonstrates that the trend, prior to America's declaration of war in 1917, was going up. The crisis catalyst changed all that. The dotted line represents what could have happened if investors had continued to buy and sell in the same way they did prior to the start of this crisis.

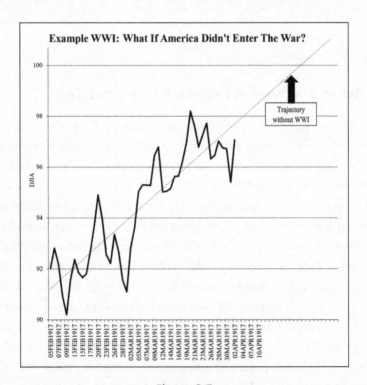

Figure 3.5

As far as cause and effect go, most people are probably not surprised to learn the Dow Jones Industrial Average dropped in reaction to the United States' entrance into both World Wars. What is surprising, however, is how quickly people change their minds. It turns out, humans are incredibly fast when it comes to adapting to the new normal.

Both World Wars took many years to conclude and the after-effects lasted far beyond the formal end of each conflict. That's a substantial time for investors to wait before they can trade again at the high market values seen before the plummet. But, in reality, the initial market drop does not last relentlessly for years. Instead, a short-term rebound allows investors the opportunity to invest/divest at generally the same levels as before the crisis ensued. Compared to the dogma suggesting investors "wait it out for years," this startling opportunity occurs quickly. To be precise, for World War II, it was just nineteen trading days after kamikaze pilots sank the USS *Arizona*, killing more than 1,100 sailors at their own dock in Pearl Harbor.

Media outlets, economists, and analysts often attempt to explain why investment markets go up or down at any given moment. It has long been commonplace to see headlines such as, "U.S. stocks open mostly higher due to strong GDP data." But these proclamations miss the simple, direct cause of the stock market's movement: the amount of purchases versus the amount of sales. What these financial headlines are actually saying is, "People are now aware of recent GDP data and we think that it's possible this information has motivated more purchases than sales, causing the market to advance." But this restatement still misses a basic truth: one cannot accurately declare a connection between investors' decisions and a specific causal event without proof that similar causal events consistently create the same reactions. In other words, are people buying because of the financial headlines or are the two things coincidently happening at the same time?

Another way to look at this is from the myriad of individual perspectives that exist in the financial world. If the financial news proclaims, "U.S. stocks open mostly higher due to strong GDP data," investors would need to, for the most part, agree that the GDP data is actually strong. Some might say it is and others might not. Additionally, investors would need to be aware of the data. Isn't it possible that there's some large number of people who transacted in the market without any knowledge at all of the GDP data? Lastly, if people truly did have consistent responses (rational or not) to regular events like GDP data or the latest company earnings report, then making a profit in the stock market would be vastly easier. Unfortunately, there is no pattern like that because there are plenty of instances when the market did not advance after strong GDP data.

But certain events do have a clear and consistent cause-and-effect relationship. If a nail tears a hole in your car tire, you'll get a flat. If a doctor shines a light in your eye, you expect your pupil will constrict. If you hear a loud, startling noise, you're likely to flinch and blink your eyes. When threatened, your body has a fight-or-flight mechanism that experience and education can minimize. Immediately after a large-scale threatening crisis begins, the Act of War Market Pattern occurs as investors sell and then turn around and buy again. In later chapters, we'll look deeper into this instinctual response, but for now, we've got a great foundation on which to build a few more basic action steps that help lay the necessary groundwork for preparing to face the next major crisis.

ACTION STEP #6: Remain calm and thoughtful to avoid emotional mistakes.

When tension turns into full-blown crisis, your ability to remain calm will affect how well you can implement many of the action steps in this book. As investors around you behave irrationally and the news describes a miasma that will last for years, it's easy to lose sight of your well-laid plans. It's tempting to join the herd, because, after all, everyone else is doing it.

Your ability to stay connected to current events and rationally use that information to protect and grow your portfolio depends on a calm approach. Many of the other action steps in this book will be impossible to implement if you, like the people in the next case study, are panicking due to air-raid sirens or picketing to have your local theater stop performing a play. Honestly assess yourself. If you're overly hot-headed or prone to excessive patriotism, you might consider delegating your portfolio management to a professional money manager or some other third party you trust.

ACTION STEP #7: Seek privacy to keep your options open.

Today, privacy is difficult to come by. We have stickers on our windshields that help highways assess tolls, and cameras on our roads record us driving by each day. Americans use social media to keep others informed of their lives and all too often "overshare" their political views and personal stances. When we face our next major threatening crisis, it could be easy for people in the grip of xenophobia or patriotism, like the ones in the next case study, to use that information against you and ultimately derail your ability to stay focused on protecting your financial future.

CASE STUDY   World Wars I and II

"Those who fail to learn from history are condemned to repeat it."
—WINSTON CHURCHILL

This case study offers you a chance to personally assess the potential challenges as you try to remain calm and seek privacy in the face of crisis. Because education and experience can help mitigate your natural impulses, try to imagine experiencing the aftermath of World War I or Pearl Harbor and steel yourself for tomorrow's crisis. How would you react if America doubled the income tax? That's exactly what happened in response to World War I. Today those tax rates look enviable, but a 100 percent increase is a radical change in any era. What if you could no longer speak the same way? Americans no longer ate German sausage or German cabbage. Instead, they enjoyed liberty sausage, liberty dogs, and liberty cabbage as people decided the word "German" had become taboo. This nation-wide change in the vernacular was a self-imposed censorship as a reaction to the Great War.

The success of the Japanese air raid on Pearl Harbor outraged an incredulous American public. Somehow Japan's military evaded the U.S. Navy reconnaissance patrols and successfully infiltrated deep into American territory, causing severe human and equipment casualties. No one alive at the time could remember a foreign attack on what would become American soil. Regular citizens felt humiliated to learn Japan's strike force consisted mostly of untrained university students motivated by family and loyalty to Japan.

Imagine the public's disgrace, fear, patriotism, xenophobia, panic, and their call for vengeance. Not just vengeance against Japan, but also for the incompetence of the leaders in Hawaii who had misunderstood orders and hobbled their own forces. The West Coast experienced the worst of this emotional tidal wave with rumors enflaming distrust of the Japanese-American population. Picture living in San Francisco where fishermen with Japanese ancestry allegedly were laying mines in nearby harbors. When you went to the grocery store, people whispered that Japanese-American farmers were lacing their vegetables with arsenic before taking them to market.

A policeman in San Jose thought he saw aircraft approaching from the sea, though no one else observed the phantom planes. Nonetheless, you'd have had to live through the air-raid sirens up and down the coast due to his report. Antiaircraft batteries were established on the Hollywood Hills, and, in San Francisco, a National Guard sentry killed a woman on the Golden Gate Bridge simply because she failed to quickly stop her car. The Rose Bowl moved from Pasadena, California, to North Carolina to avoid the local Japanese-Americans who supposedly would bomb or otherwise harm the large gathering of people. In Sacramento, someone vandalized the door of a Japanese-American Methodist Church with the epithet "Down with Japs." Police raided the Nippon Kan Theatre in Japantown and confiscated a carton of metal canisters, which turned out to be nothing but old newsreels. In one town, the city council ordered the municipal water tower be camouflaged to confuse enemy pilots.

Even without the reach of today's technology, the emotional outrage with the Japanese surfaced back then far beyond the country's west coast. For example, in Manhattan, the Metropolitan Opera announced it would not present *Madam Butterfly* again until Japan was defeated. In Washington, DC, the 104-acre Tidal Basin park containing the Japanese Pagoda, Lantern, and cherry trees was vandalized. Likely a result of the cherry trees having been a gift from the emperor of Japan, someone cut down four of them and carved the words "To Hell with those Japanese" into another. President Roosevelt himself had to veto a plan to have the White House camouflaged. The president did, however, allow antiaircraft guns to be placed on the roof despite the Axis Powers having no bomber or aircraft carrier within range of the United States capital. All of this vitriol, rumor-spreading, and canceling events is the opposite of staying calm and protecting your privacy.

When American leaders were raising money for the war effort back in World War I, they used something called the Liberty Bond, of which there were four versions. Disabled soldiers were quoted in *The New York Times* telling their parents to invest everything they could in the Liberty Bonds or Liberty Loans, as they were sometimes called. People flew planes with messages flapping behind them encouraging the purchase of Liberty Bonds. The pilots did this service out of patriotic duty and without compensation. *The Statesman*, a prominent newspaper, ran articles suggesting that people buy Liberty Bonds and listed what the country could purchase with the different denominations. Fifty dollars would buy fourteen rifle grenades or ten cases of surgical instruments. A bond for one hundred dollars would clothe a soldier or buy 2,000 surgical needles. These articles ran as "news," not in the editorial section or paid advertising. The Liberty Bond became a way to prove how citizens felt about their country, just like people proclaim their stance on social media today. Buying the bond was like wearing a badge that said something about who you were and on which side you stood. It opened people up to judge and be judged, just like what happens on Facebook and Twitter today.

In a patriotic example of irrational behavior, on May 12, 1917, approximately 75 percent of the first billion dollars in bonds was already purchased *before the conditions of the issue had been set*. Incredibly, investors were buying Liberty Bonds without knowing any of the important details about what they were buying. They were too caught up in making a statement. They had joined the herd and failed to ask rational questions like, "What was the interest rate? When would they get their money back?" Perhaps from a national viewpoint, buying bonds on blind faith with no questions asked was generally positive, but it was also not a calm thoughtful thing to do. With everyone focused on third graders writing letters to their local newspapers about the importance of buying Liberty Bonds, no one was holding their elected officials to the standard of clearly stating how the bonds would work.

And what about the people who perhaps didn't want to buy Liberty Bonds for the very rational reason that the bond offering was unclear? If they weren't private about these convictions, they'd hear the roar of the mob, accusing, "You're not a patriot like the rest of us." The fear of foreigners and the fear of people who don't have the same politics can drive many individuals to dark deeds. During World War I, masked vigilantes lynched, strung up, and killed neighbors who simply declared, "I don't like the Liberty Bond," or "I don't like our soldiers." On August 2, 1917, the world read in *The New York Times* about an "agitator" who insulted American troops and was hanged for it by six masked men. This stands in sharp contrast with the conforming neighbors who bought Liberty Bonds and were highly likely to have their names published in the local paper as a form of praise. Woe to the family next door whose name wasn't found on the printed lists because their lack of patriotism was assured and the consequences could be dire.

Just like the Americans of World War I who worried about their neighbors not buying Liberty Bonds, World War II sparked a paranoia that citizens of Japanese ancestry, and those who harbored relationships with them, were spies or saboteurs for the enemy. In February 1942, just two months after Pearl Harbor, President Roosevelt issued Executive Order 9066, which relocated all persons of Japanese ancestry. Regardless of citizenship or where they lived, those of Japanese ancestry were forcibly moved outside the Pacific military zone.

The publicly stated objectives of Executive Order 9066 were to prevent espionage and to protect persons of Japanese descent from harm at the hand of Americans with strong anti-Japanese attitudes. More than 117,000 people of Japanese descent moved as a result of Roosevelt's order, two-thirds of whom were native-born citizens of the United States. Some of these interned citizens volunteered to fight in Japanese-American combat units such as the 442nd Regimental Combat Team, which gained fame among the most highly decorated units in the war.

Today, some scholars refer to the relocation centers as concentration camps and others view internment as an unfortunate episode in a great nation's history. During the Reagan-Bush years, Congress moved to pass the Civil Liberties Act of 1988, which both acknowledged the injustice of the interned and apologized for it. The law established a cash payment for each person interned.

There's not much any of us can do about our heritage. But at least we can take the time to calmly consider how much of our lives are on display for others. Our privacy can serve as a form of protection during times of crisis and can offer a polite boundary of respect and good manners during times of tranquility. If nothing else comes of this exercise, perhaps it will make modern social media a little less divisive.

The New Normal

An overt act of war, and the conflict that follows, typically results in major upheaval. These crises are not generally over in a week or a month. The turmoil can continue for years, and the social scars can span generations. Popular opinion, and the regular advice given by

Wall Street, suggests people have no interest in buying investments during all that uncertainty and crisis-related fear. The idea is that the investing public should just hold tight while the war is waged and the crisis sorts itself out.

World War I lasted until November 1918, and its repercussions endured the next couple decades. If Wall Street's typical approach is to be believed, many would expect the market to suffer for years as investors learn of their relatives dying overseas and watch soldiers returning home to be misplaced in society. But the opposite is the case. Investors react to the crisis catalyst and quickly adjust to the new normal. The market fluctuates throughout the duration of the turmoil, and the conflict offers a number of opportunities to rational, attentive investors.

There's a story told in professional financial circles that highlights how fast we adapt to a major change. It starts with an investment advisor's longtime client describing his plan to retire at the beach where he can hear the waves put him to sleep each night. This client saves and saves, year after year, toiling away with this one thought ringing in his mind each day.

Every time the client speaks with his advisor, there's mention of the sound of the waves and how wonderful life will be in retirement at the beach. Finally, the day arrives and the client sells his house in the city and buys a condo right on the beach. That first night, he opens all the windows and has a glass of wine while looking at the stars and letting the sound of the surf crash over him. He smiles with joy realizing it's a bit difficult to fall asleep while hearing nothing but the incredibly loud waves outside.

The next day, he wakes up with happiness as first thing he hears is the waves crashing on the sand. He calls his investment advisor and tells her how thankful he is that she guided him all those years to this magical and fulfilling moment. He even holds the phone out at arm's length toward the sea so she can hear the waves, too. The days go by and the client has friends visit who all agree he has a wonderful home and the beach is beautiful.

Over time, he gets to know his neighbors and sets a midmorning appointment to go shopping with one of them. The day of the appointment, he wakes up to start his day looking forward to seeing his new friend. He opens a few windows and gets in the shower. He dresses and makes a quick breakfast, thinking he'll need to buy some more milk. And sitting at the table, bringing his spoon to his mouth, a terrible realization comes over him. Frozen, he feels a dull panic as he slowly places the spoonful of cereal back into the bowl. Turning, he looks out the window where the blue sky crowns the waves crashing among the surf.

All morning long, he'd not heard a single sound from the beach. It was as if the ocean no longer existed unless he consciously thought to seek it out. The thing he loved was there, but he'd lost that original feeling from when he'd moved to the beach. *He'd gotten used to it.* He didn't notice the ocean's sounds in the same way people no longer notice a train that goes by their home every day. He couldn't hear the waves in the same way someone can't smell a bad odor they live with regularly.

Crisis does not lead to a scenario where the markets flounder for years with no hope. Americans, and people in general, are more resilient than that because, if for no other reason, we get used to the situation. When threatening crises arise, there's plenty of opportunities to make money and grow your net worth in the stock market, and the next action step specifically focuses on how to identify them.

| **ACTION STEP #8:** Keep an Ideas List to guide your future investment efforts beyond simple war machine modernization to include the recently famous and shortage-induced disrupters.

Seven decades after World War II, unexploded bombs are still found regularly throughout Germany. They are left over from the sustained Allied bombing campaigns aimed at destroying German industry and undermining morale. In the single town of Cologne, people stop their lives to unearth and deactivate an average of twenty-five bombs each year. That's roughly 2,000 unexploded bombs since the end of the Second World War found in one small town by ordinary people like construction workers and children playing in their backyards. Over one hundred years ago, the bombs used in France in 1915 were so effective they kept children up at night in London because they could hear the explosions from across the English Channel. Germany's enemies were the first in the world to watch in terror as mines flew toward them from nearby mortars. In 1915, a new German weapon, the *Flammenwerfer*, still inspires movies and books with the horrific image of an oversized armored man carrying what looks like scuba tanks on his back, spraying liquid fire up to thirty feet in any direction he can point. However, just because a German sailor in 1915 could board the world's first 214-foot submarine and travel underwater for two hours with up to thirty-five men and twelve torpedoes, it does not mean an investor could profit from it. These are all examples of war machine modernization and not something that's easy to invest in (if you'd even want to).

The war machine can be massive, and, typically, investors give undue attention to the conflict's equipment and technology because the crisis is society's main focus. With so many people thinking it's a good place to invest, it's difficult to "buy low" and profit from those defense companies making grenades, bombs, and army boots. This means that, as you add opportunities to your list, you should look beyond the war machine to find universally good innovation.

When the next major war occurs, there will be similar weapon upgrades. Perhaps tomorrow's killer drone technology will be like machine guns or chemical weapons in World War I. Now officially banned from use by the 1925 Geneva Protocol, chemical weapons were first used in 1914, when the French used nonlethal tear-gas grenades. By 1917, mustard gas inspired the darkest of fears as soldiers in the safety of a foxhole suddenly began vomiting and writhing in pain. Weapons that performed wonderfully during World War II, but by their nature wouldn't outlast it, were many. The bouncing bomb and the famous dam buster fall into this category. Similar weaponry included the development of long-range liquid-fueled rockets such as the V-1, a flying bomb that is the ancestor of today's cruise missiles. The V-2, the world's first ballistic missile, had a range of 200 miles and a top speed of 3,500 miles per hour.

Laboratories did research to improve the war, and factories produced equipment to keep the war machine moving. During World War II, American factories produced approximately 7 million rifles, 3 million machine guns, more than 650,000 Jeeps, 300,000 military aircraft, and 89,000 tanks. By simply owning one company, General Motors, an investor could have participated in the vast majority of that wartime production; the time to buy into companies like this is during peacetime.

In wartime, the weary race for victory and the life-or-death pressure of the battlefield force people to view things differently. And occasionally those changes are universally useful. As an example, Red Cross battlefield nurses discovered the benefits of cellucotton, a very particular material created by a small American firm, Kimberly, Clark and Co. This cellucotton was found in surgical dressings during World War I. The female nurses discovered they could use it for their own personal health needs and adapted it for menstrual purposes. Not long after World War I, their adaptation was named Kotex and introduced as Kimberly, Clark and Co.'s first personal product. This was an innovation that investors could easily take advantage of by buying Kimberly, Clark and Co. when it sold shares on the public exchange in the 1920s.

The need to adapt and overcome on the battlefield helps spur forward technology and force people to try new things. Stainless steel was a British idea from World War I, which is credited to Harry Brearley of Sheffield, England. He was looking for a kind of steel to help gun barrels stay straight in spite of the heat created by the friction from rapid firing. As the metallurgist worked to find a harder alloy, some of his throwaway ideas literally ended up in the junkyard, where they lay unnoticed for some time. Brearley found that some of these discarded samples lying in the elements were not rusting, and so the secret of stainless steel was born.

The technology known today as radar came from work done in places such as the radiation laboratory at the Massachusetts Institute of Technology. Researchers created the radar equipment and devised countermeasures for it as well. Allied bombers commonly dropped thousands of tiny strips of tinfoil, called "window and shaft," to confuse enemy radar. The word "radar" didn't even exist at that time because it was originally an acronym coined in 1940 by the United States Navy meaning radio detection and ranging.

A funny example of something worth owning would be an odd plaything made by accident in 1943 that's sold over 250 million toys since. Richard James, a mechanical engineer, invented the Slinky when he was experimenting with springs he hoped could steady sensitive ship equipment at sea. Company folklore describes him accidently knocking some of his sample springs off a shelf when he somehow saw the potential for an industry-changing toy as it slowly walked down instead of falling.

Just because you add an innovation to your Ideas List, doesn't mean you're guaranteed to make money investing in it. Some of your ideas might be made by a private company and others might take a while to become well known. But take the time to stay abreast of the changes wrought by the crisis because your list is sure to be worthwhile for as long as the effects of that crisis continue to unfold. Keep the list as a guide so you don't miss a good opportunity such as owning Kimberly, Clark and Co. in the late 1920s.

The other way products or companies should get added to your Ideas List is when they become more prominent because of the crisis or war. If a company gets a government contract or has a new, nationwide exposure to the public, it needs to be added to the list. For example, in March 1941, M&M, also known as Mars, was granted a manufacturing process patent for production in Newark, New Jersey. After the United States entered the war, the candies were sold exclusively to the military because the heat-resistant and easy-to-transport chocolate complemented the American soldier's rations. By the time the war was over, millions of soldiers came home with a love for the colorful candy.

Robert Woodruff, President of Coca-Cola, demanded a bottle of Coke be made available to any person in uniform for five cents wherever he was and regardless of what it cost the company. During World War II, a special group of Coca-Cola employees, called Technical Observers, were tasked to fulfill Woodruff's vision. One hundred forty-eight men served in this role making the drink available wherever soldiers were. Two of them were killed in the line of duty. Back in the States, Coca-Cola technicians developed a portable dispensing unit easily transported by truck to any location. Nearly 1,100 of these units were used in the Pacific and allowed many servicemen and servicewomen to drink Coca-Cola in the oddest of places.

The day after war was declared, Walt Disney's Burbank, California, studio was transformed into a military installation to protect the nearby Lockheed aircraft plant. Soldiers lived in the studio and the artists had to share offices to make space. Walt Disney Productions dropped work on future projects and started creating military training films to assist the war effort and, of course, to increase the company's brand and reputation. During the war, the studio produced substantially more film projects than it did before or after with a publicized goal of education and information about the war for society. But Disney's traditional cast of characters were often featured in these short films, which ensured the cast's celebrity for years to come.

In addition to innovation, if you keep an eye out for cultural trends that will outlast the crisis, you've got your focus in the right place. As this is similar to systemic change, you can use the questions from the last chapter to help guide your efforts:

1. Does this product or service make an important part of society easier, cheaper, or faster?

2. Does this product or service provide people more freedom, more authority, or more individual capability?

3. How does this product meet a changing demand?

For example, the use of a wristwatch flourished during World War I as the pocket watch suddenly went out of style. Wristwatches were not invented specifically for the war, but soldiers needed both hands free to operate artillery barrages and other synchronized weaponry. Aviators could not take their hands from the plane controls to reach into a pocket to tell the time. The watch company H. Williamson recorded the following in its 1916 Annual General Meeting Report: ". . . one soldier in every four wears a wristlet watch and the other three mean to get one as soon as they can." One of today's most well-known luxury brands created the Cartier Tank Watch, which was inspired by the first time Louis Cartier saw a Renault tank.

After the attack on Pearl Harbor, Cadillac enjoyed the popularity created by President Franklin D. Roosevelt riding around in a heavily armored "Caddy," originally owned by the gangster Al Capone. Called the Sunshine Special, the presidential Cadillac was modified with armored plating, bulletproof glass, and submachine gun storage. Cadillac, and its parent company General Motors, benefited greatly from the car's newfound celebrity, and owners of General Motors stock were generously rewarded in the long term.

When a product isn't available during crisis, it creates a pent-up need. What company will fill that need? Throughout World War II, consumers at home experienced many shortages of basic items such as coffee, paper, rubber, and gasoline. The country imposed a national "victory speed limit" of thirty-five miles per hour to save wear on tires. Consumers had to conserve or just do without many household staples, prompting the 3M Company to run advertisements apologizing to homemakers for the scarcity of Scotch Tape in stores across the country. Available supplies of the product had been diverted to the front lines, and 3M promised in their ads that "When Victory comes, transparent 'Scotch' Cellulose Tape will be back again in your home and office . . ."

In some cases, when a product isn't available, a substitute takes its place. During World War II, plastic wrap, trademarked as Saran Wrap, became a substitute for aluminum foil to cover food. Cardboard milk and juice containers replaced glass bottles, and plywood emerged as a substitute for metal in everything from boat hulls to aircraft wings. If you keep a rational eye on commercial changes resulting from crisis, you're in a much better position to make long-term profitable moves.

In this chapter, I've explained the basic pattern that represents investors' instinctual response to a threat along with the importance of remaining calm and keeping disciplined about your privacy. These items are firsthand requirements that you cannot effectively delegate to others. But your Ideas List is easily something you could ask your investment advisor to do for you. You also could join forces with others and make a list together. In this case, it's helpful if everyone agrees to five categories that should be filled: war machine modernization, useful innovation, newly famous products, shortages and their substitutes, and, lastly, a miscellaneous category for random ideas from members of the group.

See What the Herd Cannot

Throughout this book, we'll revisit the idea that a Prepared Investor must think a little differently from the herd and see things they can't or won't. With a focus on society's reaction to a major crisis, we're going to depart from the college textbooks to see history from a very different point of view. For example, it's interesting academically that World War II should not be discussed in the past tense simply because the war is not formally over yet. Technically speaking, Japan and Russia are still in a state of war because the countries haven't signed a World War II peace treaty due to their long-running dispute over the Kuril Islands. Prepared Investors go beyond the trivia to ask meaningful questions like, "When did the crisis truly start?" and "What is the catalyst that creates a meaningful investor reaction?"

There are two more types of threatening crises: leader-driven threats and terrorism. In the next chapter, we'll examine leader-driven threats using the crises created by two American presidents as modern examples supporting four specific action steps. To set the stage, we'll go back in time to an island off the coast of France in an era when there was no internet, no telephones, and no electricity. In such a simple world, this short tale provides a stark example of how a single leader can change an entire country's government just by his very presence. In anticipation of the action steps found in chapter 4, ask yourself, "What were people's lives like just before Napoleon arrived at their front door?"

CHAPTER FOUR

Leader-Driven Threats
The Powerful Ripple Effects of Influence

The small Mediterranean island of Elba is located in the Tyrrhenian Sea about thirty miles east of Corsica. The beautiful beaches, clear water, and thermal baths attract tourists from all over the world. It's difficult to accept this paradise could have once been a prison, but for Napoleon Bonaparte during his exile from France by Louis XVIII in the early 1800s, the island was just that. Bonaparte, one of history's most recognized military leaders, commanded armies and attended lavish balls, but during his imprisonment on Elba, he and a few hundred of his loyal troops languished in humble surroundings. As a crafty bit of mockery, Bonaparte was forced to keep his title, Emperor, and a local politician offered him "the key to the city," which was just a key to the man's cellar. For the majority of 1814, Napoleon appeared a man beaten while he secretly planned his escape.

When the opportunity arrived, he chose an arduous mountain journey over the Alps, aiming ultimately for Paris where he hoped to battle King Louis XVIII for power over France. Incredibly, Napoleon and his troops successfully traversed about 120 miles on foot in the first week before finally leaving the mountains behind them. Tourists today enjoy driving what's now known as the Route Napoleon, stopping in the many picturesque, mountain villages for photos and sightseeing.

Unfortunately for Bonaparte, a small force of the king's soldiers was waiting for him just a few kilometers from Grenoble, the city where he planned to temporarily regroup after the difficult mountain trek. When Napoleon learned that the king's men were blocking his way to Grenoble, he considered his options and concluded there was no way to avoid a battle. With a quick appraisal of his soldiers, Napoleon had to accept his 600 men were walking on bloodied feet after completing the equivalent of almost five back-to-back marathons through the Alps. He knew they would rally if required, but attacking a thousand of the king's well-rested troops could only end in disaster. The only rational outcome was his arrest or, more likely, Napoleon's death.

At nine o'clock in the morning on March 7, 1815, Napoleon separated his small party into three sections, taking his place in the midst of the advanced guard, wearing his famous hat and gray overcoat. By early afternoon, Napoleon's small battalion approached the king's regiment of troops who were drawn up in a line across the road. Napoleon dismounted and ordered his men to put their weapons under their left arms, points down. Colonel Mallet, at Napoleon's side, replied, "Sire, is it not dangerous to act thus in presence of troops whose sentiments we do not know and whose first fire may be so fatal?" Napoleon repeated his order and, in testament to their loyalty, his men lowered their guns. In absolute silence, the two forces stood face to face within firing range of one another. Alone, Napoleon advanced on his horse toward the royal troops.

"Present arms!" he yelled across the empty ground. The royal troops obeyed, leveling their guns at their former commander as he slowly advanced alone, keeping his face as unreadable as possible. When he'd stopped within steps from their front line, he stared down the barrels of their guns, touched his cap and saluted. "Soldiers of the Fifth!" he cried loudly. "Do you recognize me?"

"Yes," came the resounding reply from many of the opposing troops who had served under Napoleon before his imprisonment.

"Soldiers!" Napoleon bellowed. "Behold your General! Behold your Emperor! Let any of you who wish to kill him, fire!" But this order, they could not obey. Instead, they flung themselves on their knees before Napoleon Bonaparte as if he were their savior. In that moment, using only his influence as a leader, his force more than doubled in size.

Nearly the same thing happened the very next day when Colonel Charles de la Bédoyère much larger army arrived and blocked his passage. Colonel de la Bédoyère was a cunning military strategist who had earned the loyalty of his soldiers in many previous battles. These war-tested troops had precise orders to end Napoleon's return to prominence, and they knew it would be an easy task. Facing Napoleon's smaller force on the battlefield, the colonel's experienced soldiers looked to their leader astride his warhorse and waited for him to give the order to attack. When Colonel de la Bédoyère raised his sword to give his battle cry, they did not hear what they expected.

"Long live the Emperor! Those who love me, follow me!" Colonel de la Bédoyère cried as he jumped down from his horse and embraced Napoleon on the field that, moments earlier, should have been a decisive battle and a promotion for de la Bédoyère.

By nightfall, Napoleon Bonaparte's now larger force reached Grenoble. The authorities loyal to King Louis XVIII had closed the gates to the city and the ramparts were covered with troops who had little connection to Napoleon. They confidently looked down in the failing light at Napoleon's small army. From their vantage point, Bonaparte wasn't much of a threat. That night, there would be no troops surrendering to join Napoleon's ranks. Behind their large walls, the leadership of Grenoble felt quite secure in their ability to obey their king and apprehend Napoleon.

As Napoleon's force came closer, the general populace—the peasants—took up what arms they could and attacked the gates. Armed with nothing more than farm tools and axes, their real weapon was the complete surprise of the local soldiers who personally knew these people. The soldiers did not wish to fight their neighbors, and, ultimately, the peasants' passionate efforts forced the gates open. Napoleon made his way through the gates effortlessly, passing through the crowds who had put their lives on the line for him without having been asked.

Napoleon left Grenoble on March 9, and, on his way to Paris, several regiments collected to oppose him. No battle ensued, however, because the regiments trampled their king's colors underfoot and soon began to fraternize with their friends among the emperor's troops. On March 20, Napoleon and his followers reached Tuileries Palace in Paris, the site of the Louvre today. There, they faced commanders Marshals Nicolas Soult and Michel Ney, who led the final army King Louis XVIII had sent to arrest Napoleon. But as soon as the Bonaparte's face was visible to Soult and Ney, the battle was won because, apparently glad to join their former sovereign, they immediately switched sides. The journey from Elba to Paris by Emperor Napoleon Bonaparte had come to a miraculous conclusion.

That evening, Napoleon properly completed his eighteen-day flight from exile by sitting at the king's table and eating the dinner that had just been cooked for Louis XVIII. The unpopular monarch had fled Paris just hours before Napoleon's arrival. Historians marvel at how Napoleon accomplished this change in power at the state level without spilling a single drop of blood. This is a story of how Napoleon used *influence* to regain *power*.

Reputation Versus Armies

Napoleon's secret did not lie in his heritage. He can't be called a Frenchman in the specific meaning of the word because he wasn't born in France. French was his third language, and he didn't begin learning it until he was nine years old in boarding school. The reason the French immediately experienced an astounding change of heart at just the sight of him is the influence accorded him by his experience and reputation. Once he was back in Paris at the head of the France, he had the power that comes with weapons, armies, and the ability to tax or otherwise create money.

Power indicates a leader has the ability to force others to do something, often through the use of arms. When this occurs, it is usually an overt act of war. For example, the president of the United

States has an incredible military machine that, through an act of war, can force others to fall in line with U.S. policy.

Influence, on the other hand, is the ability of a leader to sway others with words or even their very presence. Napoleon was a larger-than-life military genius with a reputation for sincerely caring about his subjects. When he put himself at the mercy of his people, offering them an authentic opportunity to kill him, he gambled on his influence with his life and was rewarded by their loyalty.

Certain people have the ability to change the course of history by virtue of their influence (whether good or bad). This means that, by saying or doing the right thing at the right time (or the wrong thing at the wrong time), certain leaders can create a crisis where the majority of people feel threatened or scared. This is different from an overt act of war in the same way that a nail in the road is different from a pothole. But the flat tire and that fight-or-flight response both result either way.

To explore a leader's ability to influence, consider the difference between President Donald Trump and President George H. W. Bush. Setting politics aside and any personal or political feelings you have for them, their ability to influence has stark differences. President Trump communicates directly to people so unpredictably, and so often, that he's created a strategic space for himself to say and do outrageous things without meaningful reaction from the public. For example, on Sunday, July 22, 2019, President Trump sent this tweet. "To Iranian President Rouhani: NEVER, EVER THREATEN THE UNITED STATES AGAIN OR YOU WILL SUFFER CONSEQUENCES THE LIKES OF WHICH FEW THROUGHOUT HISTORY HAVE EVER SUFFERED BEFORE. WE ARE NO LONGER A COUNTRY THAT WILL STAND FOR YOUR DEMENTED WORDS OF VIOLENCE & DEATH. BE CAUTIOUS!" Except for the news cycle giving it some dramatic airtime, there was little to no reaction on the part of the stock market.

The investing world didn't plummet because this tweet was just more of the same from the man who, just a few years earlier, had tweeted, "Our Southern border is unsecure [sic]. I am the only one that can fix it, nobody else has the guts to even talk about it." The spelling error aside, thousands of these messages each year creates a certain persona so that President Trump's influence will probably be felt most when he suddenly stops tweeting for two weeks.

That silence would be so uncharacteristic to his reputation, people would sit up and notice. A Prepared Investor would need to pay attention to how the public interprets that silence. If society somehow saw this aberration as indicative of a meaningful threat, it could be an example of how Trump's influence, and not his power as commander in chief, might create a crisis.

Contrast that with President George H. W. Bush who was known for being taciturn and reserved. There are many examples of Bush's understated approach to politics; one of the most dramatic occurred in June 1989, when the Chinese military used tanks, armored cars, and live fire to kill hundreds of protestors conducting a pro-democracy demonstration in Beijing's Tiananmen Square. Many in Congress cried out for a harsh punitive response to the killing of peaceful protesters, but Bush walked a conservative path. Slowly and methodically, he successfully imposed specific, almost surgical, US-Sino sanctions.

Not long after, the symbolic end of communist rule in Europe occurred in November 1989 when the Berlin Wall fell. President Bush offered a terse response at a press conference on November 9, saying simply, "I am very pleased." When the press questioned his lack of enthusiasm over the collapse of the Berlin Wall, Bush responded, "I am not an emotional kind of guy." In the short term, Bush's restrained response to the collapse of the Berlin Wall cost him among his conservative supporters who argued that Ronald Reagan would have celebrated the historic moment with some type of public address. But, in retrospect, many historians credit Bush because, by refusing to gloat about a victory over the Soviet Union, he probably helped avoid a backlash by hardliners in Eastern Europe.

Bush's conservative reputation permitted him the opportunity to address the serious challenges surrounding the process of German unification. As soon as the Berlin Wall tumbled, questions arose from all over the civilized world about how Germany should reunite the East and West. There were many proposals from various authorities such as Britain, the Soviet Union, France, and the thirty-five-members at the Conference on Security and Co-operation in Europe. If President Bush had reveled over the collapse of the Berlin Wall, perhaps the process could have ended in further conflict and bloodshed. His reputation afforded him influence, and in fewer than four months, the understated Bush Administration approved a process and brokered a deal welcomed by all.

Whether these leaders influence the world on purpose or accidentally, the question that matters to a Prepared Investor is if their action (or inaction) makes society feel threatened. As we've already discussed, when the majority of society perceives danger, it's a crisis and there is a predictable response in the stock market. Like a driver needs to look out for potholes, so too should a Prepared Investor look out for these powerful people in order to recognize that catalyst moment—that spark—when they do something to cause the stock market to drop. The next three action steps highlight how to methodically identify them and pay attention to them in current events.

ACTION STEP #9: Regularly update your list of world leaders and follow their movements.

The first step is to have a clear idea of who these people are in the world. Your list should include, at a minimum, each of the following:

1. **Political leaders such as the president of the United States and the prime minister of the United Kingdom.** There are a lot of countries in the world so at what point do you stop including their political leaders? A good rule of thumb is to gauge their weapons capability. If the country has nuclear weapons and can deliver them effectively beyond its borders, you'd want that leader on your list. This list includes the Soviet Union, France, China, India, Pakistan, North Korea, and Israel.

2. **Dictators or other all-powerful leaders,** especially if they have some animosity toward the United States. This list currently

includes Kim Jong-un, Nicolás Maduro, Bashar al-Assad, and Recep Tayyip Erdoğan.

3. **World religious leaders.** This list includes the Dalai Lama for Buddhism, the Roman Catholic Pope for Christianity, the Sunni Muslim Imam, and the two Chief Rabbis representing Sephardi and Ashkenazi Judaism.

Each year, various publications and institutions rank the most influential people in the world. The TIME 100 list is usually broken down into five categories: pioneers, artists, leaders, icons, and titans. Update your list as new rankings and directories get published.

Once your list exists, you'll want to stay up to date on what these leaders are doing because this could mean extra time for you to take action in a crisis. In the past, people would read a daily newspaper or two, but today, there are many ways to make this effort both effective and easy. For example, a simple Google Alert will provide you with a steady stream of emails whenever one of the leaders has done something newsworthy. Also in real time, Twitter and other social media give you the ability to receive updates. Unfortunately, these methods work so well that the amount of data you can expect to receive could be staggering. According to the Trump Twitter Archive, a searchable database with all the president's tweets, President Trump alone made almost 17,000 tweets in his first couple years of being president.

ACTION STEP #10: Don't let good times affect your vigilance.

Napoleon's march across France was a major crisis for the people in each town he visited. Without modern communication, the townsfolk were unaware of the threat until he was knocking on their city's front door with soldiers at his back. What were their lives like in the days leading up to the new reality in which soldiers might shoot and kill them if they somehow interfered with the invader's advance? Perhaps things were normal, even blissful and good.

There will be times in the future when this book's message will feel less urgent, just as there have been peaceful times in the past. For example, at the beginning of the 1990s, ahead of the Gulf War, American life was relatively peaceful and prosperous with many milestones in entertainment and the arts. Nirvana's album *Nevermind* and the first of the Harry Potter novels were both released at this time. *Seinfeld* and *The Simpsons* premiered and, along with *Friends* and *NYPD Blue*, the television shows helped define a generation. This was the decade of Quentin Tarantino's *Pulp Fiction* and the start of the movie franchise known as *Toy Story*.

At the beginning of the 1990s, almost no one had heard of the World Wide Web or Internet; the U.S. didn't have browsers, search engines, digital cell phone networks, or powerful laptops. But by the year 2000, Steve Jobs had made Apple a household name, and dictionaries had to update the definition of the word "Google." The United States enjoyed an economy growing at an average of 4 percent per year, and an average of 1.7 million jobs were added per year that decade.

There was so much good news, in fact, that things like a federal budget surplus and dramatic reductions in crime (murder rates declined 41 percent) were almost lost in historical footnotes. Not many recall that the unemployment rate in the 1990s dropped by half as it got down to 4 percent by the end of the decade. During this time, the median American household income grew by 10 percent, which is interesting because it has shrunk by nearly 9 percent since 2000. During the 1990s, the Dow Jones Industrial Average increased by over 300 percent, and you could still buy a beautiful Brooklyn townhouse for less than five hundred thousand dollars.

Hardly a time to be worried about catastrophe, but still the Gulf War happened and was a major crisis for the investing world. If you didn't have a plan and weren't paying attention, you'd have missed the catalyst that sparked the start of the financial pullback related to the Gulf War because it was not an overt act of war at all. And, in missing it, you'd have been swept up in the crisis and surprised when, long before anyone actually fought in the Middle East, the market dropped almost 20 percent.

It's easy for people to get caught unaware and ill-prepared when they are lulled into a false sense of security. Maybe they have a plan, but it's not worth the time that went into it if they aren't executing it. Don't let good times affect your vigilance. We'll come back to the Gulf War, but for now, the following case study puts you back in an interesting time for the United States so you can honestly ask yourself, "Would I have kept a watchful eye for the next crisis?"

CASE STUDY The Cuban Missile Crisis

"There are risks and costs to action. But they are far less than the long-range risks of comfortable inaction."
—JOHN F. KENNEDY

The decade of the 1960s was a time of significant change for America and American culture. The great amount of upheaval without gun-carrying revolution is a testament to the American dream and the ability of the national melting pot to quickly adapt and adjust. These changes were exciting, horrifying, energizing, or troubling, depending on one's individual attitude toward past traditions and beliefs. Every historical period brings some transformations, but the 1960s seemed to replace an old world with a new one. Even Americans who wanted to remain faithful to the past could not totally resist what was happening around them.

The beginning of the 1960s was a time of optimism as most Americans enjoyed economic prosperity and the collective confidence born from being one of the greatest superpowers in the world. At this time, women were flocking to stores and pouring over Sears catalogs to find a Jackie Kennedy pillbox hat. While Julia Child demonstrated new recipes on public television, women gave thought to what kitchen appliance they might purchase, such as the new microwave that was still too expensive for most families. Parents thought about moving their families to the suburbs and perhaps adding a second car. Shopping malls became more common and convenient while a McDonald's likely stood nearby offering a quick hamburger.

Literature and the arts flourished as they challenged the established traditions with new dances, television shows, and vinyl records. The Twist was popularized by Chubby Checker, and there was a variety of other youthful dances with strange names like the Jerk and the Mashed Potato. Millions of teens learned these new moves by watching their peers dance on Dick Clark's *American Bandstand*. Andy Warhol switched from commercial art to serious, realistic depictions of objects and people from popular culture. After they started playing in America in 1964, The Beatles rock group changed both music and fashion by igniting a fascination with anything British. "Beatlemania" was born on the heels of their *Ed Sullivan Show* performance, which created a music institution still influential today.

War and crisis seemed outdated as Americans changed their travel habits in the 1960s, driving their new cars more than ever. From their homes in the suburbs, family members drove to work and did their shopping. As antiquated roads became improved highways, more families vacationed by car and saw out their windows the ongoing beautification of the country. Those who stayed home watching television and reading the paper were exposed and connected to more information than ever before.

America would have its first president born in the twentieth century as a result of never-before-seen televised debates where viewers gave their blessings from their living rooms to Senator John F. Kennedy over Vice President Richard Nixon. A Massachusetts Democrat, Kennedy was handsome, self-confident, and charismatic, which meant the camera liked him and so did the voters. By the time Dwight Eisenhower, a former war hero in his seventies, turned the White House over to forty-three-year-old Kennedy, his stunning wife, Jaqueline, and their young children, Caroline and John-John, the decade was happily off and running. In fact, the country was quite literally running because of a new program JFK pushed through to try to get America more physically fit.

During these exciting, national developments, would you have remained disciplined about staying vigilant for a major crisis? If you had, you'd have been one of the few investors prepared for the short, and incredibly frightening, confrontation that could have led to a global nuclear war. The very idea of a fallout shelter didn't even exist until advocated by President Kennedy as Americans came to grip with how close they'd come to nuclear conflict in what is now known as the Cuban Missile Crisis. A standard today for tense standoffs with global repercussions, the Cuban Missile Crisis of October 1962, was a direct and dangerous confrontation between the United States and the Soviet Union, which could easily have resulted in worldwide devastation.

The crisis was unique in a number of ways, but particularly because it mostly played out at the highest levels of the White House and the Kremlin, with relatively little input from the respective bureaucracies typically involved in the foreign policy process. This makes the Cuban Missile Crisis a compelling reminder that you might not have a special view of international events. Just like the townsfolk who suddenly saw Napoleon on the hill, you'll know about the leader-driven threat right alongside the others who are paying attention to current events. This means you must remain vigilant to give yourself as much time as possible to react. Using social media and tailored newsfeeds will help the modern Prepared Investor just as brand-new televisions plugged into living room walls all across the country informed people back then.

For some readers, you already have your habits for staying current on global events. You might keep a journal, use an information aggregator like Evernote, or at least listen/read/watch the news and try to remember what strikes you as important. Others will need to relook at how they stay connected to the movers and shakers of the world. If you are starting fresh, you might use a spreadsheet with these column headings: Date, Current Event, S&P 500 value, DJIA value, and Preparation Notes. I'll provide an example of this method later in the book using current events during the COVID-19 crisis.

Back in the Cuban Missile Crisis, families gathered around *The Ed Sullivan Show* blissfully unaware that Soviet Premier Nikita Khrushchev was making a secret agreement with the prime minister of

Cuba, Fidel Castro. This agreement supplied Soviet nuclear missiles to Cuba to help deter any future invasion attempts by the United States. Construction of several Cuban missile sites was already underway when routine U.S. surveillance flights discovered evidence of the Soviet arms buildup in Cuba. With this intelligence, the president felt America would have to force the Soviets to remove the missiles and the dramatic threat they presented.

Americans simply did not know on October 16, 1962, that their nation's leadership was wrestling with how to force the removal of the missiles while avoiding the catastrophic results of war. Is the next leader-driven threat on the horizon right now and we don't know it? Is there some new information being scrutinized at the highest levels of government that is slowly moving us toward another major crisis? We can't know for sure, which is why it's important to stay alert to current events and how society reacts to them.

On the first day of the Cuban Missile Crisis, President Kennedy and other defense officials were briefed on the U-2 spy plane's findings confirming an arms buildup in Cuba. Secret discussions began on the proper response to this challenge, coalescing into two principal courses of action: an immediate air strike with invasion or a naval blockade threatening further military action. To avoid arousing public concern, the president maintained his official schedule so there was no reaction yet in the United States at the end of Day One.

President Kennedy decided to severely limit the number of senior officials informed of the enemy's missile deployment in Cuba. This small group of fifteen people was called the Executive Committee of the National Security Council (EXCOMM). His expressly stated goal was to radically restrict information to ensure neither the press, Congress, nor the general public learned about the situation until the president was ready to respond to it.

On October 17, Day Two, American military units began movement to bases in the Southeastern United States as intelligence photos from another U-2 flight showed additional proof of as many as sixteen to thirty-two missiles in place in Cuba. On Day Three, October 18, President Kennedy was visited by Soviet Foreign

Minister Andrei Gromyko, who asserted Soviet aid to Cuba was purely defensive and did not represent a threat to the United States. President Kennedy did not reveal what he knew, choosing instead to state that "the gravest consequences" would follow if significant Soviet offensive weapons were introduced into Cuba. By the end of Day Five, October 20, President Kennedy considered quarantine as a more globally acceptable form of blockade. Plans for deploying naval units were drawn up and work began on a speech to notify the American people, who still were completely unaware of the growing threat. October 21, Day Six, the president met with General Walter Sweeney of the Tactical Air Command, who explained an air strike could not guarantee 100 percent destruction of the missiles in Cuba.

Day Seven, the halfway point of the Cuban Missile Crisis, President Kennedy phoned former presidents Hoover, Truman, and Eisenhower to brief them on the situation and get their feedback. He also briefed specific cabinet and congressional leaders of the situation and informed the British prime minister, Herald McMillan, of the situation by telephone. He then summoned his closest advisors, including all the Joint Chiefs of Staff, whose advice centered on an air strike and invasion. According to Richard Reeves in his book *President Kennedy: Profile of Power*, JFK thought his generals were World War II veterans who didn't appreciate the finality of nuclear war, and said, "If we listen to them and do what they want us to do, none of us will be alive later to tell them that they were wrong."

Ultimately, the president took the suggestion of the secret EXCOMM group, and on October 22, he publicly ordered a naval quarantine of Cuba. That evening, Kennedy informed the public of the situation on national television. If you were maintaining your vigilance, you would not have missed this announcement. It's difficult to know exactly how many people saw President Kennedy's address, but records are much clearer for modern-day presidential addresses. For example, an estimated 260 million Americans did not watch President Trump's appearance in network prime time on January 8, 2019. That Tuesday evening in early 2019, about 40 million viewers tuned in, which is a lot, but not when you consider that this isn't even 20 percent of the American population.

If you would have let the good times in the 1960s dull your attention to current events, you'd have missed President Kennedy's televised explanation of the quarantine. He described in a very straightforward manner the global consequences if the crisis escalated. In homes across the United States, families heard the president sternly say, "It shall be the policy of this nation to regard any nuclear missile launched from Cuba against any nation in the western hemisphere as an attack by the Soviet Union against the United States requiring a full retaliatory response upon the Soviet Union."

A final reason to stay vigilant for influence is America's avoidance of overt acts of war today. President Kennedy specifically ensured the "quarantine" was well defined and legally not a "blockade," which would have assumed a state of war existed. This helped set the precedent for leaders trying to avoid a crisis by not making an unmistakable declaration of war. A clear and precise declaration of war requires an unwavering focus of a nation's leadership, and many historians credit President Franklin D. Roosevelt with America's final, official declaration of war during World War II. Since then, the United States has avoided labeling conflicts "wars," and instead prefers peace-keeping missions, targeted actions, systematic campaigns, sustained counterterrorism strategies, and extended military engagements. Regardless of semantics, a quarantine or a blockade, the American public interpreted Kennedy's address as a crisis.

▐ ACTION STEP #11: Make your reaction plan right now.

Most people will be unaware of the moment a leader's influence affects the stock market. For the few who did watch Kennedy's address, it still wasn't useful to them unless they'd prepared a reaction plan. What stops people from thinking ahead and getting ready for the possibility of crisis? The majority of people surely understand the importance of preparation, yet they just keep putting it off. The longer they put it off, the more comfortable they get continuing to kick it further down the road. Then the big day arrives and the plan they never made will remain so because there's only one right time to prepare for crisis. Today.

Throughout this book, the case studies and charts offer education and training. In the coming chapters, two separate Prepared Investor Profiles are devoted to walking you, step by step, through the actions one could take at the onset of crisis. Use them to help design your own action plan. But more important, note each Action Step in this book as your first act of preparation before the next crisis hits. If you seriously reflect on how you can implement each step in this book, you'll find your reaction plan has already begun to take shape.

The Act of War Market Pattern

The causal event for a Prepared Investor looking for the lopsided U formation of the Act of War Market Pattern in response to the Cuban Missile Crisis was October 22, 1962. The public instinctual reaction occurred almost immediately; as the following charts show, both the DJIA and the S&P 500 dropped sharply in response to Kennedy's evening announcement on television. When the investing public perceives a collective threat, the reaction each time is very similar. With your understanding of the Act of War Market Pattern, you'll recognize the initial drop in the market as shown next (figure 4.1 and figure 4.2 on hte facing page).

The messy U pattern after an overt act of war, which we saw in the last chapter, repeats after a leader-driven threat. For the Cuban Missile Crisis, it took less than two weeks for things to return to normal in the stock market. Before the month was over, Soviet leader Nikita Khrushchev agreed to withdraw the missiles and the major indices began a long upward march. "Both superpowers realized, after looking down that nuclear gun barrel at each other, there had to be better ways of resolving their differences," says former JFK aide Ted Sorensen. Perhaps one of those better ways was the 1963 nuclear test-ban treaty, an often-undiscussed conclusion to the Cuban Missile Crisis. A year later, at the end of October 1963, less than a month before President Kennedy's assassination, the DJIA index stood at 755.23, which was a stunning 35 percent increase. In hindsight, that chilling week was a remarkable buying opportunity, which is the norm when looking back on these moments.

CMC: Day Before vs. Day After

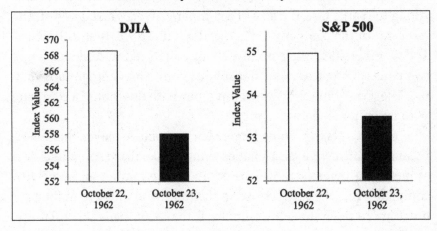

Figure 4.1

CMC: Average vs. Day After

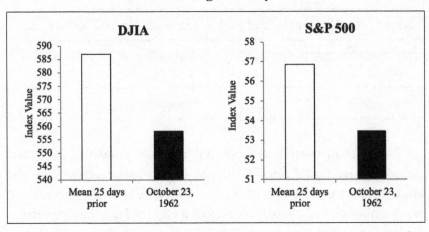

Figure 4.2

ACTION STEP #12: Recognize irrational investor behavior when society reacts instinctually to a threat.

When there's no crisis involved, people can be expected to take risk in a measurably logical way. For example, the length of time a company has existed has long been seen as a signal of their depth, their stability, and the success of their business processes over time. Along the same line, the size of a company is recognized as a strong indicator of the company's reach and ability to weather difficulties. Today, diversification is almost always analyzed in terms of larger companies being less risky and smaller companies being more volatile. The term "blue chip" is synonymous with describing a company with exceptional tenure.

From this standpoint, a larger size and tenure makes the investment more attractive, and smaller values make those companies less attractive. If investors are worried about the market and own two companies like those described in the following table, then they are much more likely to sell Company B than Company A. Volatility, also known as standard deviation, would be higher for the smaller, less-established Company B and lower for Company A.

Company A	Company B
Has been around for over a hundred years.	Just went public in the last ten years.
Worth billions of dollars—very large company.	Worth millions of dollars—smaller company.
Lower volatility	Higher volatility

For a list of companies with different sizes and different start dates, the standard deviation should be comparatively less for the larger firms than for the smaller ones. The same is true with tenure. If we examine a list of companies focusing on how long they've existed contrasted with the standard deviation of their stock price, the norm would be that well-established firms have a lower volatility than brand-new firms. The following chart (figure 4.3) provides a view of the relationship between tenure and risk where everything is rational in a pretend world of impossible perfection.

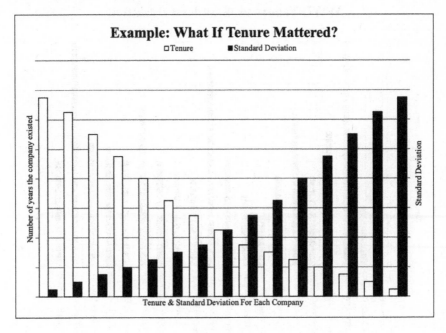

Figure 4.3

While this hypothetical chart shows what would happen if investors traded rationally, the next charts demonstrate the actual importance of tenure to investors facing the start of a crisis. In each graph, the tenure values are decreasing from left to right, which looks very orderly. But the real-world standard deviation, using values from the month after the causal event, is all over the chart without any discernible pattern. This suggests the crisis has overshadowed all rational data-driven investing.

For World War I, the next chart (figure 4.4) lists companies in the DJIA and shows their age compared to risk in the month after the formal declaration of war on Good Friday, April 6, 1917. In a clear example of the irrational investor response, the oldest company on the list, the Baldwin Locomotive Works, demonstrated a volatility far greater than the vast majority of the other, less-established companies.

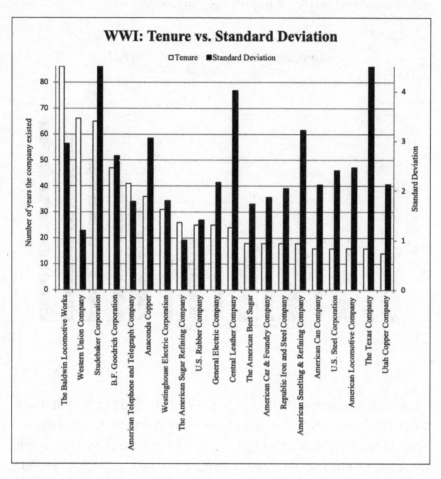

Figure 4.4

Each of these charts demonstrate that once investors saw the crisis, they didn't care anymore which companies were well established or had proven, long-term business processes. All that mattered was the fight-or-flight response. World War II reactions look very familiar (figure 4.5). The attack on Pearl Harbor happened on December 7, 1941, and the volatility of these DJIA companies had no correlation with how long they had been in business.

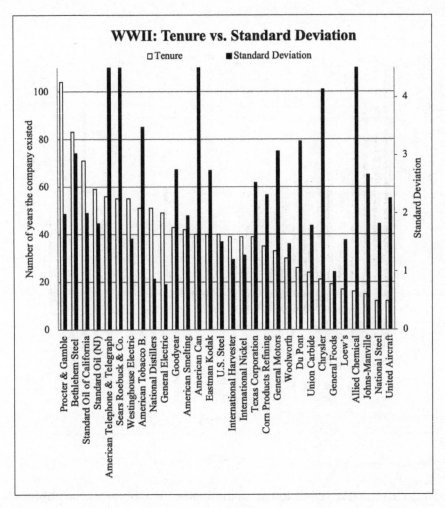

Figure 4.5

The situation was the same for the dates surrounding the televised addressed on October 22, 1962, in the middle of the Cuban Missile Crisis. In the following chart (figure 4.6 on the next page), the dark lines represent risk, and they have no discernable pattern despite the companies being listed in descending age from left to right.

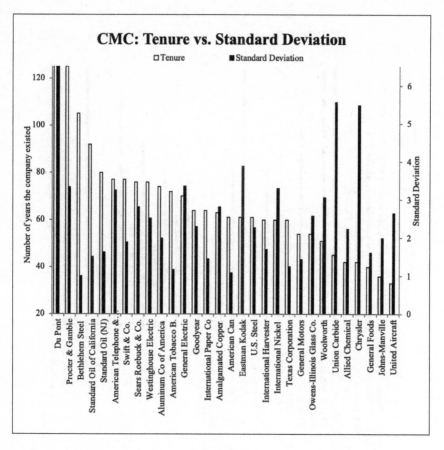

Figure 4.6

This chart suggests the main motivator for action was the public's fear prompted by their expectation of war. Clearly, investors were not interested in how long a company had been around; they only knew a crisis had occurred and immediately sold their investments. The next few charts (figures 4.7, 4.8 and 4.9) tell a very similar story except that, instead of age, it's the size, or market capitalization, of the company that is not important to panicking investors.

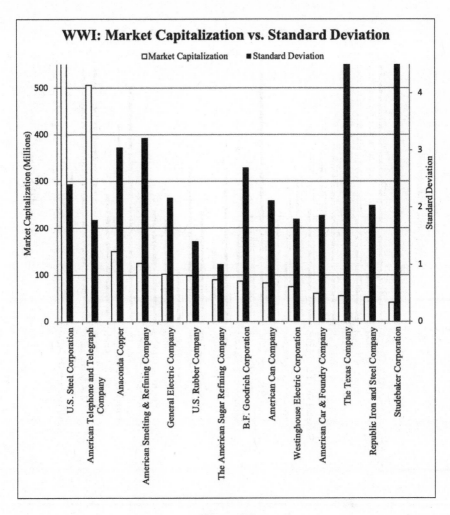

Figure 4.7

It's apparent there's no significant correlation between market capitalization and standard deviation among the list of DJIA stocks for which a historical annual report was readily accessible. The size of each company decreases from left to right using the values from those annual reports (figure 4.8 on the following page).

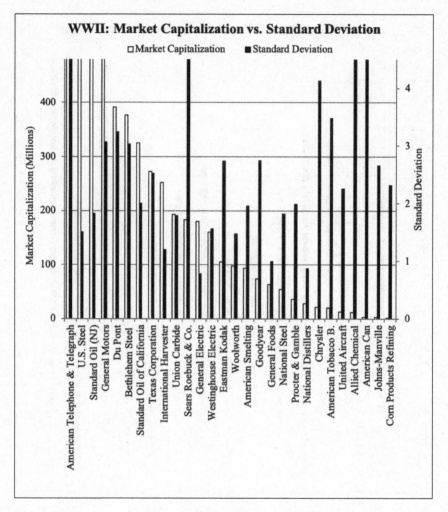

Figure 4.8

The risk, or standard deviation, associated with each company should get larger from left to right. Instead, there is such a lack of correlation, that only one conclusion makes sense: the size or history of a company just doesn't matter to the investing public immediately after the start of a threatening crisis (figure 4.9 on facing page).

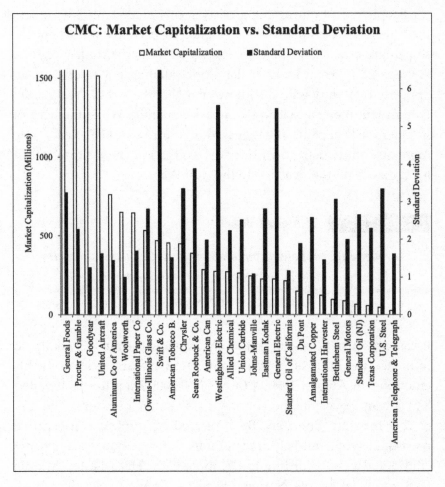

Figure 4.9

As seen, the volatility of the position during a crisis does not cor-
respond with either the size or the age of the companies. If people
behaved rationally and weren't selling with only the war in mind,
they'd sell less of the well-established firms. Because the standard
deviation does not track with a company's size or age, investors were
not measuring the market as they typically do. Instead, they were
reacting instinctually with the all-consuming certainty that accompa-
nies crisis. War! Crisis! Sell! And then just a short time later, the new
threat became less worrisome as people got used to the new normal.

People react to threatening crisis in this predictable way unless they have the training and experience to permit them to choose something other than the response given to us by Mother Nature. A Prepared Investor looks at share prices falling due to crisis as an opportunity to buy with the knowledge that the Act of War Market Pattern will inevitably lead them back up again. While the herd of investors sells in panic, the Prepared Investor buys. Let's look at one more case study using the leader-driven threat that was the catalyst for the stock market reaction to the Gulf War.

CASE STUDY The Gulf War

"Leadership is a potent combination of strategy and character.
But if you must be without one, be without the strategy."

—GENERAL NORMAN SCHWARZKOPF

President Bush's lack of showing emotion meant his ability to influence the start of a crisis came from making a show of his emotions. In August 1990, a force of 100,000 Iraqi troops invaded Kuwait and overran the country in a matter of hours. The day of the invasion, President Bush offered his typical conservative reaction, saying publicly that military intervention wasn't being considered yet. According to Dr. Richard N. Haass, a top Middle East specialist on the National Security Council, President Bush meant it was premature to seriously entertain a military response. The press, however, interpreted President Bush to mean he had taken a military response off the table, when in fact he had not. This misunderstanding frustrated President Bush greatly, but America didn't know that yet.

The day after Saddam Hussein's invasion of Kuwait, the president began a process of meetings in places like Aspen, Colorado, and Camp David. He or his emissaries met with the British prime minister, Margaret Thatcher; General Norman Schwarzkopf; Deputy Secretary of State Lawrence Eagleburger; Secretary of Defense

Dick Cheney; Secretary of State James Baker; the Soviet foreign minister, Eduard Shevardnadze; and General Colin Powell, chairman of the Joint Chiefs of Staff. The president returned from Camp David on Sunday, August 5, and as soon as his helicopter touched the ground, Dr. Haass huddled with him to go over the latest, most pressing issues. He described the president as frustrated with the press, who seemed too quick to criticize his administration for not doing enough. After the heated discussion near the helicopter, President Bush stalked over to the eagerly awaiting White House press corps and unloaded one of the most memorable and emotional phrases of his presidency: "This will not stand, this aggression against Kuwait!"

What if President Bush had not been so emotional? The next chart (figure 4.10) offers a dotted line to show how trading might have continued if nothing had changed from the previous two months. There's clearly some nervousness that might be related to the invasion, but the index hadn't left its recent trading range.

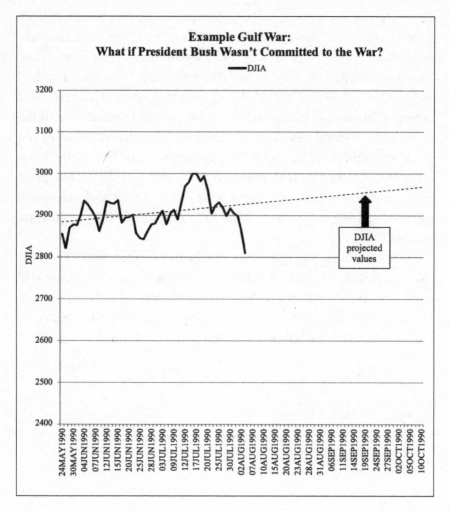

Figure 4.10

This expressive departure from the norm was the spark that blazed into a serious decline in the Dow Jones Industrial Average. Until then, the Dow Jones Industrial Average had been knocking on the door of a 3,000-point milestone value, but had stopped twice just a fraction of a point away in the month before the invasion. The following chart (figure 4.11) graphically shows the start of the Act of War Market Pattern. Bush's comment that Sunday meant a lot to investors even though it was not an actual declaration of war.

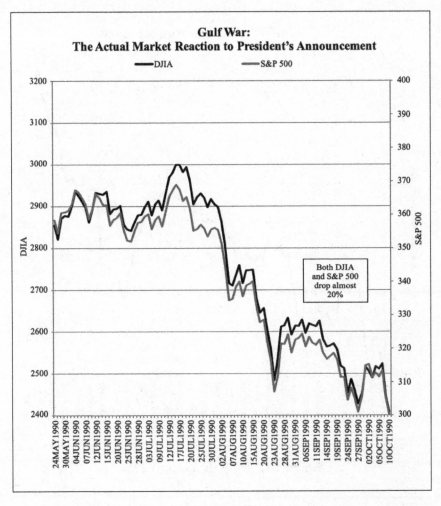

Figure 4.11

Here is the rest of the Act of War Market Pattern (figure 4.12 on the following page). The second half of the U-shaped curve takes a little longer than previous examples, but the pattern remains the same.

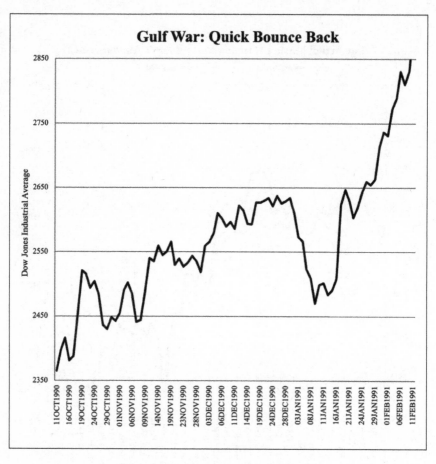

Figure 4.12—DJIA rises almost 23%

The following chart (figure 4.13 on facing page) looks extremely similar to what we've seen from other crises in the previous chapter.

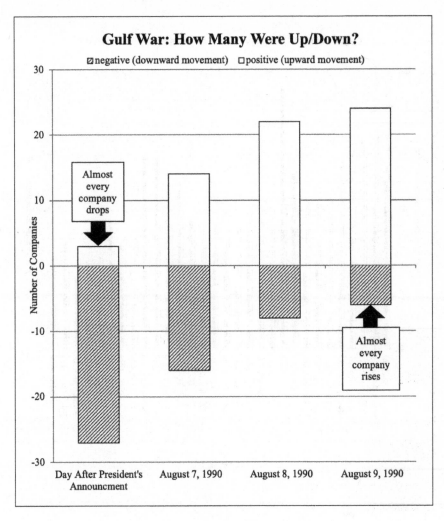

Figure 4.13

As expected, investors were not thinking about basic, rational data when they were buying or selling during this time. Regardless of the age or the size of the company, investors participated in their typical reaction to the threatening event (figures 4.14 and 4.15 on the following page).

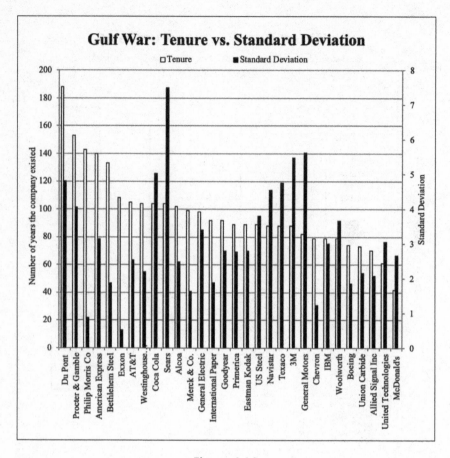

Figure 4.14

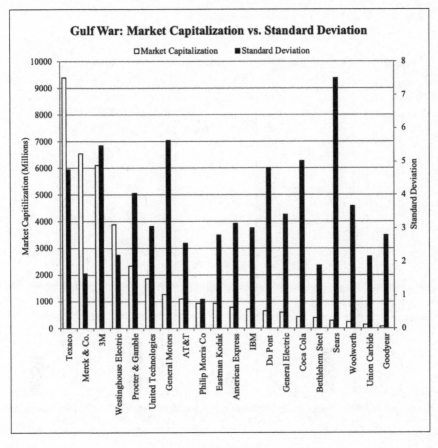

Figure 4.15

Just like we examined in the Cuban Missile Crisis, the day before the catalyst and the day after paint a very clear picture of people selling their investments after Bush's announcement. August 3, 1990, was a Friday and the announcement occurred on Sunday. Monday, August 6, is the next trading day for this analysis (figures 4.16 and 4.17 on the following page).

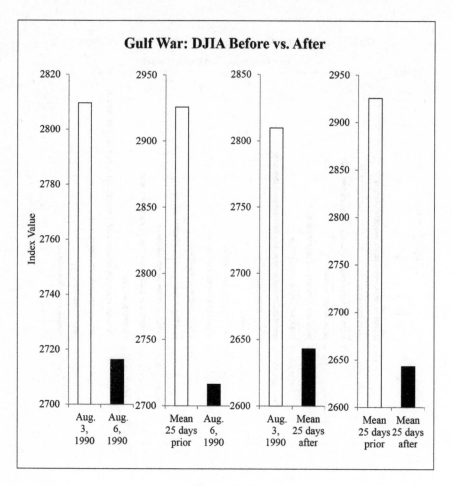

Figure 4.16

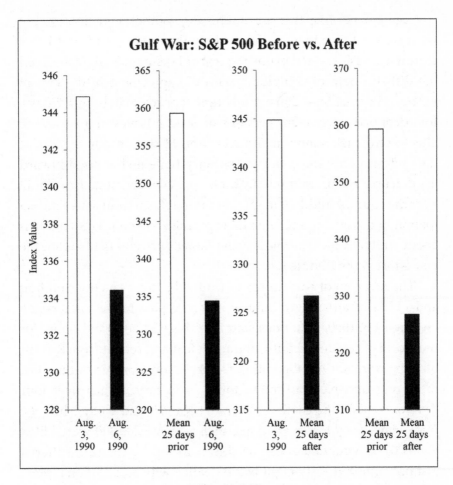

Figure 4.17

True to his understated reputation, President Bush relied on his experience in foreign affairs to create a global coalition committed to compelling Iraq to withdraw. There was a problem that arose when the administration realized that if Israel joined the coalition, it would alienate the Arab countries who had already joined the alliance. President Bush made a request to Israel's leadership that proved both his influence and their humble commitment to the United States when they agreed both to stay out of the coalition and to refrain from retaliating if they were attacked.

Agreements like this are interesting footnotes in history, but what makes this one incredible is how the entire country of Israel endured a crisis created by the request of President Bush. They lived the difficult path of complying with the agreement in the face of serious personal loss. During this time, approximately thirty days, Iraq dropped thirty-eight versions of Scud missiles in a variety of attacks on Israel, mainly in Tel Aviv and Haifa. Despite the loss of life and property, the country's military remained focused inward on defense, repair, communication, and coordination. Israelis all over the country huddled in safe rooms to refrain from active participation in the war and to keep their promise to honor U.S. concerns about Arab coalition partners using Israel's activity to abandon the war effort in the Middle East.

The invasion of Kuwait led to United Nations sanctions on Iraq and a U.S.-led air and ground war. For a Prepared Investor, it began on August 5, 1990, with Bush stating, "This will not stand," and, for the world, it concluded with an Iraqi defeat and retreat from Kuwait on February 28, 1991. Operation Desert Storm was one of the most rapid and decisive wartime victories in history. In just over four days of combat, the coalition liberated Kuwait and vanquished the Iraqi army. Iraqi losses were massive, as some 200,000 were killed and 600,000 wounded or captured. U.S. forces, by contrast, suffered just one hundred forty-eight battle deaths, with an additional ninety-nine suffered by their coalition partners in one of the most lopsided results in military history.

After the catalyst for the Gulf War, the DJIA dropped from August 3 to October 10 as the index moved from 2,809.65 to 2,407.90. The S&P 500 reacted similarly as the index dropped from 344.86 down to 300.39. But those losses did not last years as some might suggest. Instead, overall indices returned to pre-war levels in about six months. What's more, of the twenty-seven DJIA stocks that dropped on August 6, almost half of them had bounced back *in less than six trading days*. People were quickly comfortable with the fresh information and the situation was no longer new.

Once the indices come back to prewar levels, the Act of War Market Pattern is over and the collective reaction is complete. At that point, the markets are no longer predictable due to the crisis. The market might go up or it might languish for years; the point is, we're back to the new normal. But, for a brief moment, investors experience real fear and unconsciously form up with the herd in their response to a threatening catalyst. For both the Cuban Missile Crisis and the Gulf War, the market dropped and then the indices rose again, permitting investors to buy or sell investments as if Presidents Kennedy and Bush had never said or done anything at all.

From the Gulf War's start to its finish, the United States had a lot of good news on the progress in the Middle East. But every crisis is not so cheery. Acts of terrorism are usually followed by hard-hitting updates as the effects of the attack slowly become known. The aftermath of terrorism can be mistaken for additional crisis catalysts because each new piece of news feels like another shock to the public. In chapter 5, we'll examine the importance of not mistaking crisis aftermath for a crisis catalyst and the detriments of doing so. We'll examine presidential assassination and explore the beginnings of 9/11 in a case study designed to further prove the importance of preparing right now. We'll also use your knowledge of the Act of War Market Pattern to provide an example of how an investor could use that pattern in real time to protect and grow a portfolio.

CHAPTER FIVE

Acts of Terrorism
Both Foreign and Domestic
How to Separate from
the Investing Herd

W hen dropping my teenager off at our neighborhood driving school, there was a group of other students waiting for the instructor to arrive. My attention was captured when I heard one of the young ladies exclaim, "I almost died!" Over the next few moments, I listened as she described how a police car pulled up behind her on the shoulder of a highway. She was very open about being intimidated by the flashing lights as she watched the officer get out and approach where she was standing near the trunk of her car. She was clearly distraught that she had frozen completely and was physically unable to speak to the officer. Suddenly, one of the other student drivers interrupted her.

"But wait, why were you on the side of the road?"

"Oh yeah, I had a flat tire."

The aftermath (a policeman showing up) of a crisis (a flat tire) can be both overwhelming and intimidating. Part of separating from the investing herd in the face of crisis requires us to not only stay calm but also keep moving in the right direction. We cannot freeze up or get distracted by the natural repercussions that follow a catastrophe.

If Prepared Investors can identify the crisis catalyst, they can use the Act of War Market Pattern to protect and grow their portfolio. Because an act of terrorism, by definition, is the crisis catalyst, the challenge is not in identifying it. Rather, the difficulty is in remaining aloof from the herd through the dramatic, and often horrifying, aftermath. The panic, the media coverage of past events, the on-site accounts of what happened, the accusations, the finger-pointing, and the unfounded assumptions can be overwhelming for the unprepared. In the weeks that follow, much of the "news" is actually further description of what led up to the act of terrorism or new, messy details designed to heighten drama and capture your attention. But, from a portfolio management standpoint, this is only noise.

John Paul Jones, the American soldier, said, "Whoever can surprise well must conquer," but our capacity for surprise is limited. Whether it's a bombing or your portfolio management, there's only one shot at the element of surprise. We get used to things so quickly that it's normal, natural even, for the untrained masses to turn their focus to new information instead of dwelling on the original event. Let's do an easy exercise to drive this point home. I challenge you to imagine four or five shocking scenarios you believe will be surprising no matter the circumstances. It could be anything from, "An alien lands in the backyard," to "I see Benjamin Franklin walking down the street."

Don't read ahead now. Stay with this exercise, and try to really think about your scenarios and choose a surprising situation big enough that it will still be shocking no matter the setting. While you consider which of your ideas is the most terrible surprise, I'll commit to offering you just one setting that makes every shock you imagine go away for investors. No matter what you've come up with, my single set of circumstances will completely neutralize your entire list of surprises. Here's a clue to how easy this will be: think back to the story of the client who retired to the beach back in chapter 3.

Are you ready for your terrible surprise to be neutralized? Add these words after any shocking scenario: ". . . just like every day last week." Here's my own list of terrible surprises with the additional phrase added:

. . . came home to a surprise party . . . just like every day last week.

. . . got pulled over for speeding in a school zone . . . just like every day last week.

. . . couldn't move my arms and legs . . . just like every day last week.

. . . a plane flew into a building . . . just like every day last week.

. . . saw Sasquatch . . . just like every day last week.

Because we naturally adapt so fast, the crisis catalyst quickly gets lost in the crisis aftermath. When something bad occurs, our instinctual reaction is, "OK, that happened. Now, why did it happen? How did it happen? Who's most affected? What's the new situation because of it?" It's normal for the investing herd to get swept up in the aftermath questions of a crisis, particularly an act of terrorism, and a Prepared Investor needs to stay focused on the catalyst rather than on the resulting fear and anxiety (which mostly comes from learning new information about what already happened); otherwise, you risk making poor choices that could hurt your finances.

Of the catalysts that make society feel threatened, an unambiguous one is the assassination of a country's leader, such as John F. Kennedy. When a leader is killed in cold blood, it creates a unique kind of uncertainty. People are shaken and scared, and our understanding of who we are as Americans is threatened. It doesn't matter if you'd voted for JFK or not. The fact that the most powerful person in the country was vulnerable to murder shines a light on our own vulnerability.

Many Americans today still feel the loss of John F. Kennedy, who was sworn in as the thirty-fifth President on January 20, 1961. At his inaugural speech, he challenged Americans to be active citizens with his still-famous request, "Ask not what your country can do for you, ask what you can do for your country." He was the youngest president elected to office at age forty-three years and 236 days, as well as the youngest to leave office at forty-six years and 177 days.

Many books and movies have depicted the scene in Dallas on November 22, 1963, when John F. Kennedy waved to cheering crowds from the open top of a Lincoln Continental. The day before, he'd flown to Texas to give several political speeches. If all had gone well, he'd have spent the weekend relaxing at Lyndon Johnson's ranch. Instead, America watched in horror as shots were fired, and, within a few hours, police arrested Lee Harvey Oswald. But none of those books or movies are simply a description of the assassination by itself. People are instinctively drawn to the why, the how, the who, and the drama that ensues.

ACTION STEP #13: Don't mistake "more bad news" as a new, or second, crisis.

Fear and anxiety heighten as people keep getting bombarded with new information describing in more and more detail what happened. Most crises, but especially acts of terrorism, provide a slow feed of new heart-wrenching particulars and horrifying follow-up events. For example, the public didn't learn for some time that when the assassination happened, the president's wife, Jacqueline Kennedy, refused to change out of her blood-stained pink suit. She reasoned, "I want them to see what they've done." Even more alarming, a second murderer, Jack Ruby, shot and killed Oswald two days after the assassination, silencing the only person who might have offered more information about the tragic event. Hundreds of thousands of people gathered in Washington for the president's funeral, and millions throughout the world watched on television.

Yet through all the detail describing where the bullets struck him and how his wife reacted, the stock market movement shows the Act of War Market Pattern began when America's leader was suddenly murdered, not from any of those post-crisis tragedies. The threat investors perceived originated from the shooting in Dallas, not from the ripple effects of the assassination in the days that followed. In the following two charts (figures 5.1 and 5.2 on the next page), you can see that people sold their investments immediately upon learning of the assassination. The resulting aftermath, while emotionally charged and very distracting, does not derail the natural reaction of investors to the original catalyst.

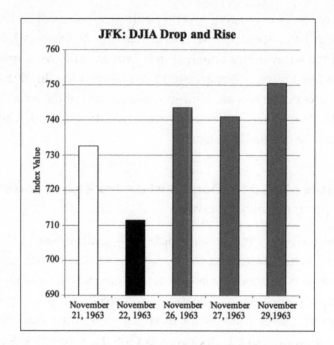

Figure 5.1 (above); Figure 5.2 (below)

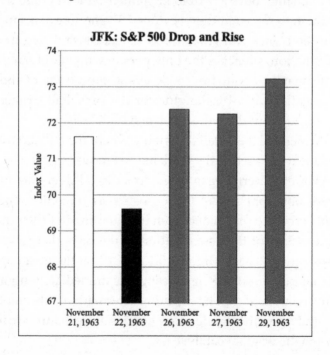

The Dow Jones Industrial Average and the S&P 500 decisively fell after the assassination of JFK. While the stock market was open on Friday, November 22, 1963, the New York Stock Exchange closed early at 2:07 p.m., just twenty-six minutes after the media reported that Kennedy had been shot. The American Stock Exchange quickly followed the lead of "the big board" and halted trading activity at 2:10 p.m. Trading was closed, as usual for the weekend, but it remained closed on Monday, November 25, 1963, for the funeral of JFK. At that point, there was no way to predict if investor sentiment was going to continue to drive down the market, but a Prepared Investor would be comfortable with the fact that, at some point in the near future, it would come back and complete the U-shaped formation. As it happens, the indices recovered on that Tuesday, November 26, 1963.

Dan Millman, TEDx speaker and author of *Way of the Peaceful Warrior*, says, "Timing is everything." He's right. When the next crisis hits, it's important to recognize the difference between the catalyst that galvanizes investors as opposed to all the aftermath that follows. When the public becomes aware of a major act of terrorism, such as watching their president get assassinated on television, that's the most important data point a Prepared Investor uses to gauge the start of the investing herd's natural reaction to a threat.

All of the following news—and it will be horrible—is aftermath, and the markets absorb that into the Act of War Market Pattern, which occurs very quickly after a threatening crisis strikes. Investors' natural reaction begins with people selling their investments, which, in turn, causes the market to drop. At this point, all the public cares about is the perceived collective threat, whether real or imagined. Rational data doesn't matter. There is a trading day, as demonstrated in the next chart (figure 5.3 on the following page), when most investments rise, even if they don't get back to pre-crisis levels. In less than six months, the market rises to pre-crisis levels, and, following the assassination of JFK, it was done in less than a week.

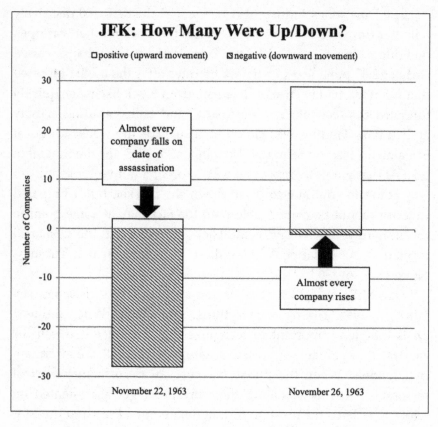

Figure 5.3

The moment the news reported live about a second plane crashing into the World Trade Center in New York City, the nation became aware of the nature of the tragedy on September 11, 2001. As the news walks backward from any singular act of terror, it takes us through many different perspectives and individual stories that will be plastered everywhere as a result of the attack. Sometimes it's a very long and dramatic wait before a picture forms from the many tragic pieces and the calamity can be beheld in its entirety. Each of those pieces cannot be publicly known at once in real time, but instead they get "discovered" and reported on in the aftermath.

Examining any act of terrorism would support the importance of making your action plan right now so you're not caught unprepared.

But in addition to being a surprise, the aftermath from this kind of crisis can easily be mistaken as another catalyst for an additional crisis, making it hard to separate from the investing herd and execute rational portfolio decisions. When the next act of terrorism occurs, the results of the attack—damage and loss of life—will be broadcasted as one would expect, but there's also the story of how it happened. Even though "how it happened" occurred in the past, each detail comes out to the public in a chaotic manner, presented like it's fresh and new.

A Prepared Investor needs to understand that this news is not new; otherwise, you'll misunderstand where the Act of War Market Pattern truly begins. The investing world is not immune to the panic and fear blazing high as a result of all the probing, digging, and torturous dripping of shocking details in the news cycle. A Prepared Investor responds to the act of terror itself and stays aloof from the resulting aftermath because the subsequent information, revelations, and awful data do not warrant starting all over again with your investment plans.

The following 9/11 Case Study follows a logical timeline, but real life will not present these details to you this way. As you read ahead, try to imagine each detail as a randomly presented, separate headline that grabs the public's heartstrings and, compounding fear on top of worry, finally steals away their sense of logic. Each new development such as intel on the terrorist pilots, transcripts of passengers' final phone calls, or the uselessness of America's early warning system feels like another fresh and horrifying problem. In real time, these facts bombard the public sporadically and, therefore, incoherently. But none of the follow-up information serves as a catalyst in the way the actual attack does. After America knows it happened, that's your catalyst and it's the only one. Your action plan unfolds based on that moment, not what happens after. Later in this chapter, I'll give you a step-by-step example of how a Prepared Investor might have reacted to 9/11. For now, immerse yourself in the details of 9/11 for a glimpse of what you might expect to see and feel after the next major crisis.

CASE STUDY   **9/11 Terrorist Attacks**

"We will remember every rescuer who died in honor. We will remember every family that lives in grief. We will remember the fire and ash, the last phone calls, the funerals of the children."

—PRESIDENT GEORGE W. BUSH

The 9/11 tragedy did not begin on September 11, 2001. Historians look as far back as February 1998, when Osama bin Laden published a *fatwa* in a London-based Arabic newspaper calling for the murder of any American, anywhere on earth. This focus on "an evil America" gained traction as the months went by, and bin Laden's apparatus for identifying and recruiting the right operatives for a special mission gained strength. These men all made their way by various methods to different places in the United States throughout 2001. In fact, on August 13, it appears some of them held a planning session in Las Vegas led by Mohamed Atta, a forty-three-year-old pilot from Egypt who had graduated from Cairo University in 1990 with a degree in architectural engineering. Twenty-nine days before the attack, Atta accompanied Marwan al-Shehhi in Las Vegas where they prepared to take control of one of the planes during the attack. Other hijackers were in Florida that same day, while a third and final team was in Minnesota. As part of their preparation, the Florida-based hijackers bought silk shirts and khaki pants at department stores in Pompano Beach ten days before the attack so that they could blend in better on the day of boarding. Zacarias Moussaoui, an al-Qaeda recruit in Minnesota, raised some suspicions when he requested training on a flight simulator at Pan Am International Flight Academy, but for some reason had no interest in earning a license.

The hijackers had a few systemic advantages that worked greatly in their favor. First, the element of surprise was on their side because of their unique method of using airborne commercial planes to execute the attack. An added advantage was the difficulty converting names from the Arabic alphabet into English because often there is no single correct spelling. That is why the names of the suspects vary in different news accounts and why computerized databases don't recognize a terrorist's name if it is spelled differently from how it was originally entered into the database. For example, Mohamed can also be spelled Mohammad, Muhammad, or Mohammed. Additionally, the hijackers were not young fools, blindly acting out their jihadist religious fever. To the contrary, they were all similar to Mohamed Atta's associate, Abdul Aziz al Omari, a Saudi Arabian who attended the Hamburg University of Technology, Germany, where he earned an electrical engineering degree.

From three different areas of the country, the hijackers planned to take four flights on Tuesday, September 11, 2001. They were the 7:45 a.m. American Flight 11 from Boston, the 8:00 a.m. United Flight 175 from Boston, the 8:00 a.m. United Flight 93 from Newark, and the 8:10 a.m. American Flight 77 from Washington, DC. The terrorists operated in five-man teams though there were only four hijackers on United Flight 93 from Newark. The operative likely intended to complete the team for this flight, Mohamed al Kahtani, had been refused entry by a suspicious immigration inspector at Florida's Orlando International Airport earlier in August.

The terrorists intended to attack quickly after each flight took off, and all the teams accomplished this successfully. On United Flight 175 from Boston, the hijackers attacked sometime between 8:42 and 8:46 a.m. They used knives, mace, and the threat of a bomb as they stabbed members of the flight crew and likely killed both pilots. As the hijackers took control of the planes, people around the nation began to receive calls from passengers and officials inside the aircraft. The last thing the world heard from inside this first plane from Boston was a flight attendant exclaim over the phone, "We are flying low, oh my God, we are way too low." Just twenty seconds before 8:47 a.m., American Flight 11 from Boston crashed into the North Tower of the World Trade Center in New York City. All passengers onboard and an unknown number of people in the tower died instantly.

Opposite the hijackers that day stood the American authorities like the Federal Aviation Administration (FAA), the FBI, and the North American Aerospace Defense Command (NORAD). From their point of view, notification of any hostile attack from the air begins on the eastern slope of Colorado's Front Range mountains where the Cheyenne Mountain hides installations for NORAD, the Air Force Space Command and the United States Space Command. The fifteen three-story buildings in this hollowed-out mountain were erected amid miles of tunnels to create an underground complex of over four acres designed to survive a direct hit by an atomic bomb. The facility is entered through fifty tons of doors that are three-feet thick and can automatically swing completely closed in less than twenty seconds. Guarded and closed to the public, the Cheyenne Mountain operation center tracks every man-made object entering North American airspace. It is the heart of the nation's early warning system and is rumored to be able to detect the firing of a long-range missile anywhere in the world before the missile has completely left the launchpad. But all this capability was utterly useless against domestic aircraft launched from within the nation's air travel system and then turned into flying weapons.

Twenty-four days before the attack, Special Agent Harry Samit of the FBI submitted a memorandum from Minneapolis to his headquarters in Washington requesting a court order permitting him to search a terrorist's computer. His memo stated Zacarias Moussaoui was conspiring to commit a terrorist act, but it went unread by Michael E. Rolince, FBI Section Chief, International Terrorism Operations Section. One of the FBI's leading al-Qaeda experts, John O'Neill, might have read the memo, but he was dealing with his own problems arising from *The New York Times* story about a misplaced briefcase, which unfortunately forced O'Neill to resign.

Outside Washington on September 10, electronic intercepts at the headquarters of the National Security Agency picked up conversations between two suspected al-Qaeda leaders. One read, "The match begins tomorrow," and the other, "Tomorrow is zero day." These conversations would not be translated or transcribed until September 12. None of the airport supervisors or screeners reported anything suspicious that morning or recalled the hijackers when interviewed later by the Federal Aviation Administration (FAA).

The first indication of a problem occurred just before 8:25 a.m. when Boston Air Traffic Control Center heard someone aboard American Flight 11 attempt to communicate with the passengers. The microphone used was not an internal intercom for the plane, and it's doubtful the hijackers were aware they were broadcasting to the nearby tower in Boston when they said, "Nobody move. Everything will be OK. If you try to make any moves, you'll endanger yourself and the airplane. Just stay quiet." Air traffic controllers in Boston heard the transmission, but the passengers on the plane did not.

The air-traffic-control radar-beacon system is a sophisticated and complex method of communicating and tracking planes as they move from place to place. Each plane has a unique code that helps airports confirm important travel data. The first operational evidence indicating something was abnormal on the second flight from Boston, United Flight 175, occurred at 8:47 a.m., when the aircraft changed beacon codes twice within sixty seconds. At 8:51 a.m., the flight deviated from its assigned altitude. and a minute later, New York air traffic controllers began repeatedly and unsuccessfully trying to contact it.

At 8:54 a.m., American Flight 77 from Washington, DC, deviated from its assigned course to turn south. Two minutes later, the transponder was disabled just before losing primary radar contact. Indianapolis air traffic control repeatedly tried and failed to contact American Flight 77 from Washington. Dispatchers from American Airlines also tried without success. By 9:00 a.m., American Airlines Executive Vice President Gerard Arpey learned communications had been lost with American Flight 77 from Washington. This was now the second American Airlines aircraft in trouble, so he ordered all American Airlines flights in the Northeast not yet in the air to remain on the ground. His decision was probably the first official reaction from within the system of various authorities in the United States.

A crisis of this nature had never occurred in the United States, and it had been more than thirty years since anyone in the world had seen anything similar. On the day of the attack, no one at the FAA

111

or the airlines had ever dealt with multiple, coordinated hijackings where the terrorists' goals were both mass murder and self-destruction. In this light, leaders at the airlines and in government agencies were reasonable to assume that other aircraft in the air weren't also at risk. As news of the hijackings filtered through various official channels, there was no cause yet to consider grounding every plane in American airspace. Instead, individual FAA controllers, facility managers, and command center managers at the local levels had to fight up the chain of command to convince leaders to recommend a nationwide alert to stop all air traffic. It took some time before every commercial airplane in the United States was finally grounded.

Long before the nationwide grounding, the second plane from Boston, United Flight 175, struck the South Tower of the World Trade Center at 9:30 a.m. This second collision rippled through the national media while all passengers on board and an unknown number of people in the tower were killed instantly.

For those who remember 9/11, this was likely the moment they felt the first uncertainty, the first tremor of fear. The terrorists had accomplished something horrible, and the facts presented thus far would come out chaotically in the days and weeks after the attack. Today, an entire generation does not remember this event because they are too young. For them, this is all as unreal as the next major crisis will be to each of us. When the next unforeseen act of terror occurs, part of being prepared is having a plan ready for how to react and, just as important, not letting additional negative news in the crisis aftermath derail that plan.

Every crisis is unique in some way. It's this newness that helps inspire fear in the investing herd. At the highest levels of the United States, questions about which nation-state to hold responsible were very difficult to answer and the unidentifiable enemy made the destruction even more difficult to accept. George W. Bush, America's forty-third president was transformed into a wartime president in the aftermath of the airborne terrorist attacks. His father, also a wartime leader, believed responding to the terrorism of 9/11 was the greatest challenge of any president since Abraham Lincoln.

That morning, President George W. Bush was in Sarasota, Florida, where he'd gotten up early for a morning run. When American Flight 11 from Boston struck the World Trade Center at 8:46 a.m., no one in the White House or traveling with the president knew it had been hijacked. While that information circulated within the FAA, there is no evidence the hijacking was reported to any other agency in Washington before 8:46 a.m. As a result, the presidential motorcade arrived at Emma E. Booker Elementary School in Sarasota without pause, and President Bush began to read to a class and talk about education. White House Chief of Staff Andrew Card was standing with the president outside the classroom when Senior Advisor to the President Karl Rove first told them a small engine plane had crashed into the World Trade Center. The president initially thought, like many around the country, the incident must have been caused by tragic pilot error. Before entering the classroom at 8:55 a.m., the president spoke to National Security Advisor Condoleezza Rice, who was at the White House. She recalls telling the president about the twin-engine plane, stating it was a commercial aircraft that struck the World Trade Center, adding "That's all we know right now, Mr. President."

At the White House, Vice President Dick Cheney had just sat down for a meeting when his assistant told him to turn on his television because a plane had struck the North Tower of the World Trade Center. The vice president wondered how such a tragedy could have occurred when he saw on his television screen the second aircraft strike the South Tower. By 9:34 a.m., Ronald Reagan Washington National Airport advised the Secret Service of an unknown aircraft, now identified as American Airlines Flight 77 from Washington, heading in the direction of the White House.

At the Pentagon, Secretary of Defense Donald Rumsfeld was having breakfast with some members of Congress, after which he returned to his office for his daily intelligence briefing. The meeting was interrupted so he could be informed of the second strike in New York. He resumed the briefing while awaiting more information. Meanwhile, American Airlines Flight 77 from Washington had turned from its intended flight path and was five miles away from the Pentagon when it began descending past 2,200 feet, pointed toward the Pentagon and downtown Washington. At 9:37 a.m., an Air Threat Conference Call began that lasted more than eight hours. The president, vice president, secretary of defense, vice chairman of the Joint Chiefs of Staff, and deputy national security advisor all participated in this phone conference at various times, as did military personnel from the White House underground shelter and the president's military aide on Air Force One.

At almost the exact same time the conference call started, the hijacker pilot advanced the throttles to maximum power and American Airlines Flight 77 crashed into the Pentagon, traveling at approximately 530 miles per hour. Those who survived, including Donald Rumsfeld, the powerful secretary of defense who had served under multiple presidents, immediately began assisting with rescue efforts on the property and in the parking lot. Ultimately, everyone aboard the plane and an unknown number of civilian and military personnel were killed on the sixtieth anniversary of the groundbreaking of the Pentagon.

Victims, fatalities, heroes, casualties, prey, martyrs, losses, targets, passengers, noncombatants . . . Rather than identify a single word to summarize what befell the people on the front lines of this terrorism, it's easier to describe what they were not. They were not soldiers. They were not enemies of Islam. Like all innocents in the crosshairs of terrorism, they were not deserving of harm.

They were people like Amy Sweeney, an American Airlines flight attendant, who, at 8:25 and 8:29 a.m., called from American Airlines Flight 11 from Boston to calmly report that the plane had been hijacked. She explained that a man in first class had his throat slashed and two flight attendants had been stabbed. Her straightforward report described a flight attendant with a serious injury who was on oxygen while other people's wounds seemed minor. Importantly, she had the presence of mind to relay the flight attendants' inability to contact the pilots and how a terrorist had said there was a bomb in the cockpit. This was the first of several occasions that

morning when various flight attendants took admirable steps outside the scope of their training because they could not communicate
with the cockpit crew.

Five minutes after the hijacking began, Amy Sweeney's
coworker, Betty Ong, contacted American Airlines Southeastern
Reservation office in Cary, North Carolina, via an AT&T Airfone to
report an emergency aboard the flight. The emergency call lasted
approximately twenty-five minutes, as Ong calmly and profession-
ally relayed information about the events taking place aboard American Airlines Flight 11 from Boston. At 8:19 a.m., Ong reported, "The
cockpit is not responding. Someone is stabbed in business class, and
I think there's mace. We can't breathe, I don't know, I think we're
getting hijacked."

In Easton, Connecticut, a man named Lee Hanson received
a phone call from his son Peter, a passenger on United Flight 175
from Boston, at 8:52 a.m. His son told him, "I think they've taken
over the cockpit. An attendant has been stabbed and someone else
upfront may have been killed. The plane is making strange moves.
Call United Airlines, tell them it's Flight 175 Boston to LA." Mr.
Hanson then called the Easton Police Department and relayed what
he heard. A few moments later at 8:59 a.m., passenger Brian David
Sweeney tried to call his wife, Julie, and was able to leave a message
saying the plane had been hijacked on the family's home answering
machine.

At least two callers from United Flight 93 from Newark said the
hijackers knew the passengers were making calls but did not seem to
care. Five separate calls helped the outside world piece together how
the passengers on Flight 93 intended to revolt against the hijackers.
According to one of the calls, they actually voted on whether to
rush the terrorists and attempt to retake the plane. At 9:57 a.m., the
passenger assault began, and a terrorist in the cockpit named Jarrah
immediately began to roll the airplane to the left and right in an
attempt to knock the brave passengers off balance. At 9:58 a.m., Jarrah told a hijacker in the cockpit with him to block the door. At 10:01
a.m., Jarrah stopped the violent maneuvers and exclaimed, "Allah is

the greatest, Allah is the greatest." He then asked, "Is that it? I mean, shall we put it down?" His coconspirator replied, "Yes, put it in and pull it down."

The passengers continued their assault, and, at 10:02 a.m., the hijackers screamed, "Pull it down! Pull it down!" The terrorists remained at the controls but likely believed the passengers were only seconds from overwhelming the cockpit. That's when the airplane nosed down, the control wheel turned hard to the right, and the airplane rolled onto its back. One of the hijackers began shouting, "Allah is the greatest! Allah is the greatest!" With the sound of the passengers' counterattack continuing behind him, Jarrah plowed United Flight 93 from Newark into an empty field in Shanksville, Pennsylvania, at 580 miles per hour, about twenty minutes away from Washington, DC, and the White House.

All of America is a 9/11 survivor, but some bear more of the burden than others. Harry Waizer is one of a small cadre of people who worked at the brokerage firm Cantor Fitzgerald before the attack and, as of this writing, still works there. A tax lawyer, Mr. Waizer was on an elevator on his way up to work when the first plane struck and flames engulfed him. Badly burned, he stumbled out onto the seventy-eighth floor and worked his way down. Despite doctors giving him a 5 percent chance of survival, he spent two and a half years recovering and ultimately returned to work in 2004. His scars are still visible, and he cannot sit for long periods during his shortened work week. In a 2011 *New York Times* article, "The Survivor Who Saw the Future," Waizer told Suzanne Craig, "Cantor Fitzgerald is a different company today, some of the employees who just joined were just teenagers in two-thousand-one. Some of the employees are children of the parents who died that day."

When American Airlines Flight 11 from Boston struck Tower One, Howard W. Lutnick, the head of Cantor Fitzgerald lost more than desks, files, and future revenue. Three of every four people who worked in New York City for Mr. Lutnick died that morning, including his younger brother, Gary. With 658 people dead, Cantor Fitzgerald, perhaps more than any other company, symbolizes the horrors of September 11, 2001. In the number of employees who died, it has no rival. Almost one-fourth of the 2,753 people killed in New York City worked for Mr. Lutnick.

Beyond the World Trade Center and New York City, the entire country was perhaps more affected than it had been when JFK was assassinated. One can look as far from Manhattan as Central Florida where the Walt Disney Company closed its stateside theme parks that morning. The guests were forced into the streets of the park because all the rides were closed, and then park employees held hands to form a smiling human wall that guided the guests from the park. This procedure was done at all four Walt Disney World Parks, and guests were given complimentary tickets at the turnstiles as they left.

Some companies that didn't yet exist were unable to ever form because of 9/11. For example, the gyroplane, a helicopter that can take off almost vertically and fly 330 miles at a cruising speed of 320 miles per hour, was invented prior to the terrorist attacks. Different from an actual helicopter, a gyroplane uses a gas turbine-powered propeller to drive the craft forward and to power two asymmetrical overhead blades. In the summer of 2001, test flying was proceeding according to plan, and the FAA certification program progressed as orders for the aircraft came in. With plans in place for production, the investment funds and future success seemed assured until the terrorist attacks devastated the aviation industry.

For me, this case study was one of the most difficult parts of writing this book. Editors and beta readers have shared with me that they were "triggered" by this short exercise, which was precisely the point of including the intricate details unfolding that day. This information was trickled out over a period of days and weeks, not all on the day itself. If merely reading these accounts can cause a change in pulse, imagine what happens when emotions are high in real time. It's normal to feel fear and panic. When it's happening around you and not just a historical recounting, you, as a Prepared Investor, will stay focused on the catalyst that started it all. Everything else, however heart-wrenching, is an effect, not a cause.

Final Development of the Act of War Market Pattern

You're now familiar with the three types of threatening crisis: overt acts of war, leader-driven threats, and acts of terrorism. You know that, by identifying the crisis catalyst, you can expect to see a particular pattern in the stock market that represents the natural human response to a threat. You know that the pattern looks like a lopsided U as the market falls and comes back over time, usually in less than sixty days. We've discussed the importance of being calm and maintaining your privacy as you actively look for opportunities to add to your Ideas List. President Kennedy would have been on your list of influential leaders, and your vigilant attention to current events means you'd have been ready to take action in light of his assassination. You understand that investors don't react rationally because they sell their investments without paying attention to the age of the companies or the size of the companies. All that matters to them is the crisis, and 9/11 was no different.

The markets fell in value almost immediately, and, if you use the 9,605.51 value of the Dow Jones Industrial Average the day before the terrorist attack as a benchmark, the intraday low of 8,755.46 on the following Monday is significant. On the first day of trading after the attack, the market closed down 684 points, a 7.1 percent decline, which is one of the biggest losses in New York Stock Exchange history for one trading day. As the week concluded, the Dow Jones Industrial Average was down almost 1,370 points, representing a loss of over 14 percent and an estimated $1.4 trillion in just five days of trading. The following charts (figures 5.4 and 5.5) demonstrates how the actual public reaction wasn't a slow decline over the next year or even six months. The market dropped fast just like it had in previous crises discussed in this book. In just ten days after the terrorist attack in New York City, the market's drop was done. September 21 marked the event low point and was only the fifth day the stock market was open after the terrorist attack, though almost two weeks had passed.

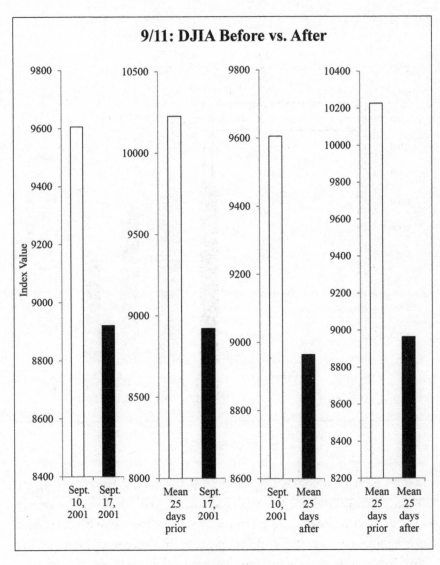

Figure 5.4

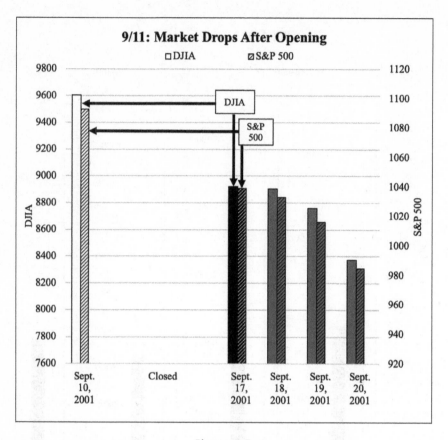

Figure 5.5

The next two charts (figure 5.6 on the facing page and figure 5.7 on page 122) show the first half and second half of the messy U shape that follows a threatening crisis. It drops like a rocket and rose again just as fast. While 80 percent of the components of the Dow Jones Industrial Average dropped on September 17, the vast majority of the declines reversed back to pre-9/11 values within just nineteen days. From September 20 to the end of the year, the major indices rose approximately 20 percent.

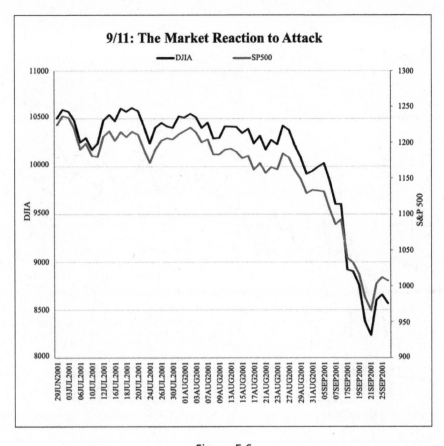

Figure 5.6

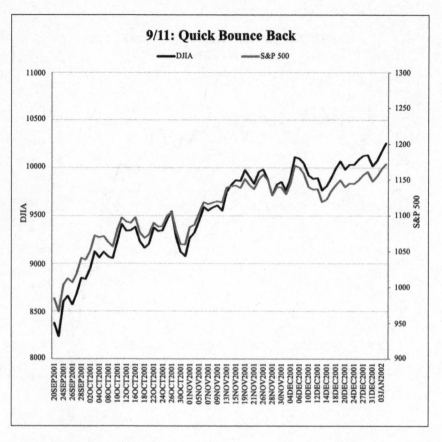

Figure 5.7

Similar to reactions in past crises, there is a day, shortly after the catalyst, when almost all stocks in the Dow Jones Industrial Average rise together as investors adapted to the new situation (figure 5.8 on the facing page).

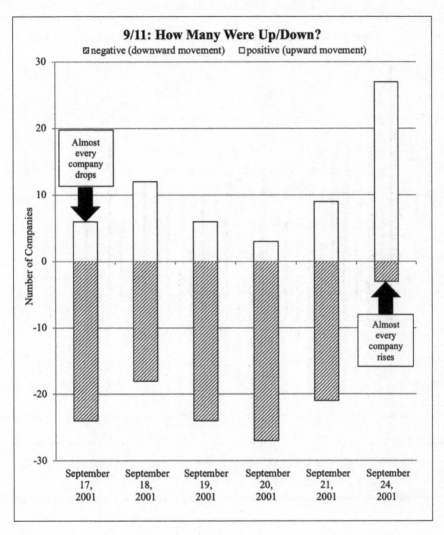

Figure 5.8

It doesn't matter whether it's 2001 or 1963, the following charts (figure 5.9, 5.10, 5.11, and 5.12 on the following pages) show that neither the tenure nor the size of the thirty Dow Jones Industrial Average companies had much bearing on their volatility as investors thought only about the crisis.

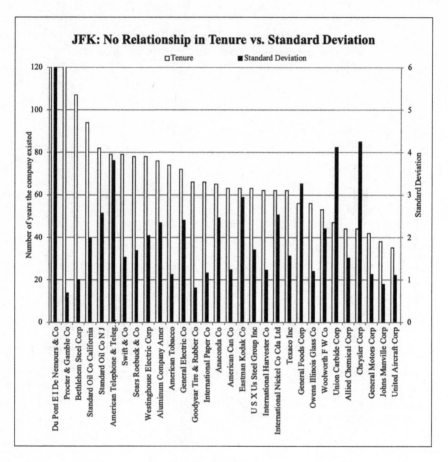

Figure 5.9

With such an intense focus on only the crisis, size and tenure is almost meaningless. Does that mean that everything is meaningless in the face of crisis? Do investors just sell in panic-driven fear without regard for anything else at all? No, they do not. The crisis consumes their attention, which means that any company perceived as directly related, or immediately affected, will have magnified effects on their short-term stock performance. For example, the overall market dropped a bit in late September 1982 when a few people

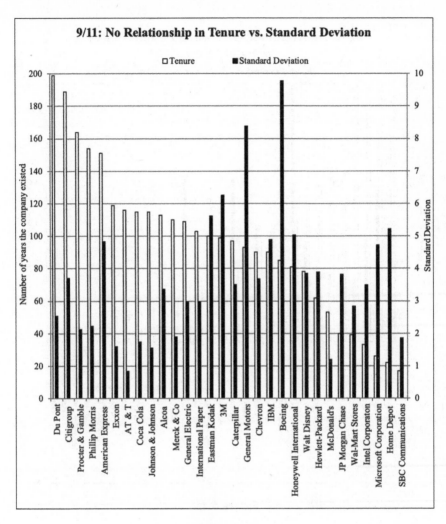

Figure 5.10

in Chicago died from ingesting potassium cyanide. The poison was found in Tylenol capsules, a Johnson & Johnson product. If investors saw nothing but crisis and were simply selling everything in blind panic, then all companies would fall about equally. But that's not what happened. In reality, Johnson & Johnson fell dramatically more than other companies because of the obvious connection between the crisis and their product.

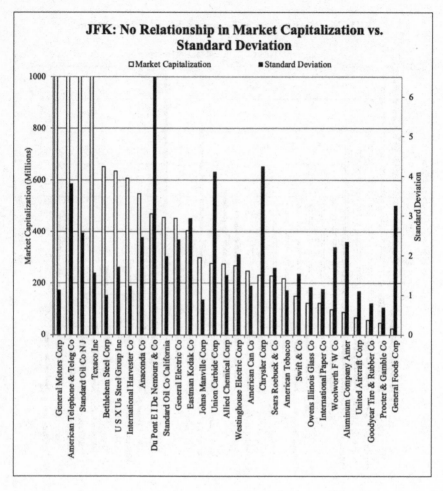

Figure 5.11

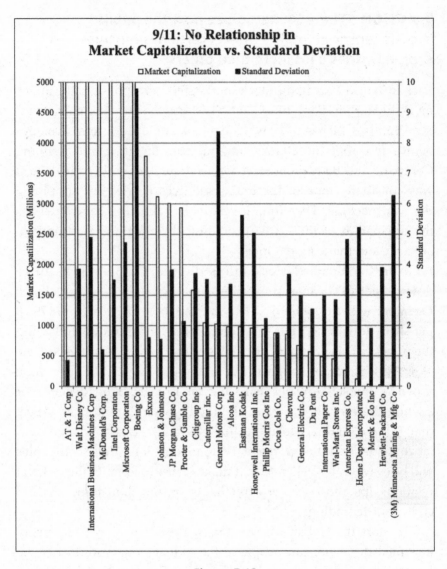

Figure 5.12

ACTION STEP #14: Recognize how the public's crisis-centric mentality affects certain companies or industries a lot more than others.

Back in World War II, the stock market fell in response to the attack on Pearl Harbor. For a time, that crisis was the only thing on investors' minds, which is why, when we look at the short-term averages before and after the attack, the American Smelting and Refining Company and Bethlehem Steel *did not drop*. For World War II, steel was considered one of the main resources needed for supplying the war machine. Therefore, investors bought the steel companies in anticipation of the crisis, providing them with opportunity to advance and make more money.

Which companies' stock prices did panicked investors drive down after 9/11? American Airlines, trading on the New York Stock Exchange with the symbol AMR, watched its stock drop from $29.70 per share down to $18 per share on the first day of trading following the attacks. This was a 39 percent decline. United Airlines, on the New York Stock Exchange as UAL, dropped from $32.82 per share down to almost $17.50 per share that day in a 42 percent decline. For a while, there's only the crisis, and the Prepared Investor can expect that, if there's a direct relationship between the crisis and a particular company or industry, the market movement for those companies will be exaggerated. Therefore, it makes sense to identify those direct relationships and consider capitalizing on the short-term wave of crisis-centric trading.

To start the Cuban Missile Crisis, President John F. Kennedy informed the American people of the military quarantine after the New York Stock Exchange had closed on October 22, 1962. Therefore, October 23 is the day the stock market strongly reacted. It's evident how investors were thinking because every company in the Dow Jones Industrial Average went down except for the few firms focused on copper, steel, aircraft, and aluminum. Whether right or wrong, the public saw only the potential for war and blindly acted on the perception those particular industries would be the only profitable investments during the crisis ahead. Even though we've seen, crisis after crisis, that the market as a whole does not languish in loss for years, investors still react as if only the crisis-centric industries will be able to make money.

As a last example of this crisis-focused reaction, let's look at the Gulf War (figure 5.13). Though individually unaware that they were driving the market through a messy U shape in late 1990, investors cooperated together as if they'd been practicing the Act of War Market Pattern for years. But not every company in the Dow Jones Industrial Average fell. When starting with the closing bid price on Friday, August 3, 1990, all stocks in the Dow Jones Industrial Average—except three of them—dropped on Monday after Bush's announcement. What do these three companies that did not drop have in common? Oil.

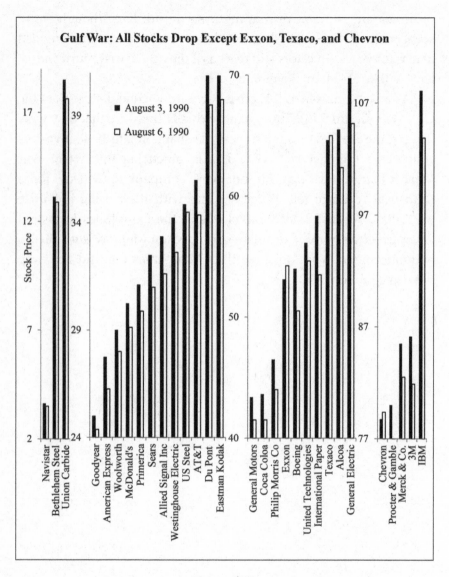

Figure 5.13

130

Prepared Investor Profile:
Sally Smith and Her Portfolio Actions during 9/11

"By failing to prepare, you are preparing to fail."
—BENJAMIN FRANKLIN

A typical investor today, Sally Smith is a nurse living in Texas. She has two investment accounts she can view online, and, with the help of an independent financial advisor she's known for years, she tracks her portfolio by looking at it once or twice a month. She knows about diversification in general and is comfortable buying investments, with the expectation they will go up in the long run. She recently inherited some money after her mother passed away, and she now has a total of about $1 million, all invested in various stocks, bonds, mutual funds, and exchange traded funds. She understands how margin works, and, since her portfolio has margin capability, Sally employs it on rare occasion when she and her advisor agree the situation warrants the use of market-secured debt. She knew the 9/11 terrorist attacks were a major crisis and, because she read this book, she understood to expect the Act of War Market Pattern. Without *The Prepared Investor*, she probably would have done nothing or maybe she'd have sold along with the panicking herd.

But Sally Smith did not panic. She'd already had an in-depth discussion with her investment advisor about each of the steps in this book and knew she wanted to meaningfully and decisively act when the next crisis hit. As part of the plan they'd agreed on, she was not going to try to profit from trading in any individual companies that could be directly affected by a future crisis. Therefore, after the Twin Towers fell in New York City, she was looking for the first step in the Act of War Market Pattern—a drop in the market—and she was ready for it. The following timeline shows what she could have done with her portfolio using real dates and market values surrounding the 9/11 terrorist attacks.

September 11, 2001: The second plane strikes the World Trade Center, and Sally Smith's coworkers tell her what is happening. She's at work and cannot do anything immediately to manage her portfolio.

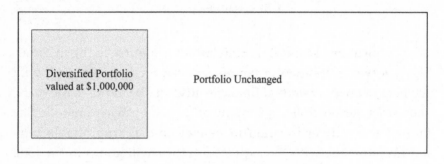

Figure A1. Sally's Overall Portfolio

September 12–14, 2001: Sally has to work each day and uses her free time for family plans and 9/11-related communication to friends and loved ones.

September 15, 2001: Sally logs into her portfolio or reaches her financial advisor, and takes two decisive steps related to her expectation that she'll see an Act of War Market Pattern. The first step she takes is to determine the pre-crisis market value of the S&P 500 was 1,092. Second, she decides her entry point will be 7 percent below that at 1,016. The market isn't open so she continues to wait.

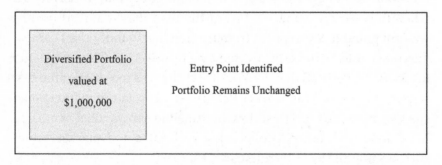

Figure A2. Sally's Overall Portfolio

September 16, 2001: Because Sally Smith's portfolio is fully invested in a diversified manner, she doesn't want to sell anything to make a purchase. Therefore, she decides to utilize her margin capability when the market opens tomorrow. She chooses to buy $300,000 worth of an ETF that moves with the market at three times the volatility. With her financial advisor's help, she places an order to make the purchase when the S&P 500 gets down to 1,016.

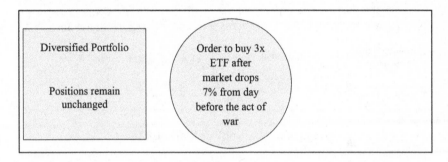

Figure B. Place Order to Buy ETF Then Waiting for Market to Fall

September 17–20, 2001: The market opens and the plummet begins. Her order executes sometime before close of business on September 20. She now owns an ETF that tracks with the S&P 500 index providing three times its return.

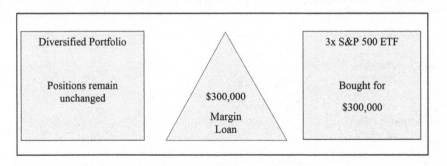

Figure C. Buy Order Executes

September 21, 2001: Sally and her financial advisor prepare to sell the investment when the S&P 500 index has risen to 1,087, which is about 7 percent up from her purchase point. If that movement occurs, she expects a return of approximately 21 percent due to the multiplying nature of the ETF she bought.

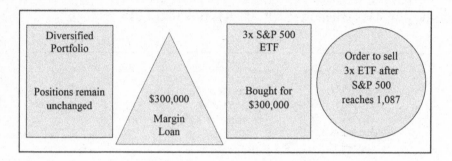

Figure D. Waiting for Market Rise

October 11, 2001: By this date, her advisor has sold the position, meaning both the ETF and her margin loan are gone. Her $300,000 investment yielded more than $60,000 in profit, but we'll use $60,000 for simplicity and to help account for variables such as imperfect ETF tracking, margin cost, and transaction fees. For her portfolio overall, she's earned a nice profit that can help cushion any future blows to her traditional, well-diversified portfolio.

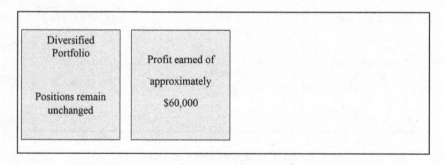

Figure E. Sell Order Executes and Margin Loan Is Gone

November 2001: Sally Smith looks over her September and October statements to confirm everything happened the way she wanted it to. The entire process yielded a portfolio return of approximately 6 percent in only about thirty days. She now has a sizeable cash position she can use to make purchases if she and her advisor wish to take advantage of any future market dips.

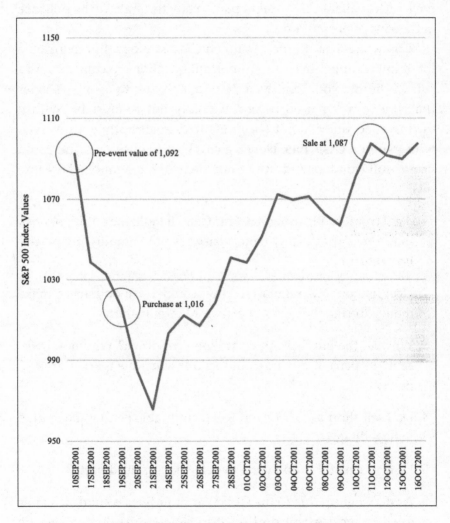

Figure F. Sally Smith's Response to 9/11.

135

▌ ACTION STEP #15: Know your risk tolerance.

Is Sally Smith's approach the right way to do it? Is it the best way to do it? This completely depends on your willingness and ability to take risk with your portfolio. For some, the best action might be to liquidate the majority of their portfolio at that high point, which marks the end of the Act of War Market Pattern. For others who have cash available, they might plan to buy throughout the pullback at the start of the pattern.

Like a chess game, there is no one best strategy. But there are a lot of interesting moves and important questions to consider. As a rule of thumb, you don't want to suddenly use tools or strategies that you've never used before. If you're not comfortable with it during good times, don't feel pressured to abruptly get involved with it after a crisis hits. Here's a checklist of questions you could use to fully understand how your own risk tolerance plays into this:

1. Am I comfortable using margin? Can I handle the additional risk that comes with using market-based debt to amplify my portfolio's return?

2. Do I use options regularly? How could I use options to make money during the next Act of War Market Pattern?

3. Why set the purchase price at 7 percent down? Why not 9 percent? 14 percent down? Could I do it when the market drops 3 percent?

4. Do I sell short regularly and feel comfortable betting the market will go down?

5. How much of this do I want to delegate to a third party?

6. As oil went up due to the Gulf War or airlines went down after 9/11, to what extent do I want to focus my efforts on specific industry or company movements?

7. As I fill my Ideas List from chapter 3 with companies and products that could become money makers, what portion of my portfolio should I commit to those buys?

8. How much cash do I have? How much of this savings am I willing to commit to helping protect and grow my net worth in times of crisis?

9. If I wish, can I raise more cash ahead of the crisis? How much of my current portfolio is locked up behind backout fees or long-term contracts?

10. How much do I have to make so that I'm still on track for the goals that are important to me?

For beginning investors who would like a good place to start, here's an excellent one-size-fits-all approach that addresses these questions. First, don't try to profit on the downturn at the start of the Act of War Market Pattern. Like Sally Smith, use that time to get ready to take action. Don't use complicated strategies that you're not used to yet like options trading, trading on margin, short selling, or other more sophisticated approaches to the stock market. Instead, buy broad-brush, index-style investments that capture a lot of the stock market at once. When you buy, be ready for the market to keep dropping. It's okay if you didn't buy at the exact moment that it starts to go back up. Also, be ready for it to go up a bit and then fall further as the days go by. If you identify where you want to get in and out, then you've done a great job copying what made Sally Smith so successful.

In the next chapter, we'll walk through another example of how to manage a portfolio in the face of crisis, except we'll use an accredited institutional investor with a bit more risk tolerance and a lot more investment experience than Sally Smith. We'll also explore how society's perception influences the action steps in this book. If society sees a crisis, then there is one . . . even if there's not.

Often, the framing—how a situation or circumstance is positioned to be received by the public—produces noise and distractions that throw investors off track by making them see a crisis that isn't there. The opposite is true as well. This has happened a lot in our nation's history, which is why assessing society's experience and making a connection between the stock market and how a crisis is framed are important skills a Prepared Investor must hone. The next chapter teaches you how.

CHAPTER SIX

Social Assessment
How to Read the Room and Accurately Gauge Investor Panic

I f this book's focus thus far has been on human behavior in relation to crisis, then this chapter sheds light on what drives that behavior. Knowing how the public receives the news as major events unfold is just as valuable to a Prepared Investor as identifying the conflict itself. Consider for a moment the adage, "It's not what you say, it's how you say it." When it comes to our fears as a species, the instinctual response is greatly influenced by these three things: the basic facts, the "meaning" of those facts, and the fear of the unknown.

In plain speak, the "how you say it" part is called "framing." Conflict specialists refer to the term "framing" to mean the process of describing and interpreting an event. How a situation is framed makes all the difference in the way people conceptualize the problem and its solutions. They receive the basic facts, but their understanding of them is dependent upon how the information is framed. What does it *mean*? Is it good or bad?

Also called framing bias, one of the most famous examples was put forth by Mark Twain in his book *The Adventures of Tom Sawyer*. Tom had to whitewash a fence, and he presented the situation to his friends as though they were being excluded from the joyful happiness of painting the fence. Using Tom's lens to view the facts, his friends felt unlucky that they'd missed the chance to whitewash the fence, and they solved that problem by giving Tom some of their personal treasures for the "opportunity" to do the chore.

139

Conflicts themselves can be a call to action, but how a conflict is framed can make the difference between mass hysteria and complete indifference. Prepared Investors understand fundamentally that the way society conceptualizes a situation matters because, for a catastrophe to affect your portfolio, the majority of society needs to act in concert. From that point of view, your ability to accurately gauge society's perception is an extremely important part of being financially prepared for the next crisis.

It's useful for a Prepared Investor to be able to identify an actual threat from a terrorist or an overt act of war, but that's relatively easy. Accurately reading the room—watching society as it watches a crisis—is a lot more difficult because there are times when society won't respond to very real danger and, in contrast, times when the public panics due to lack of experience and fear of the unknown. I will explore two concepts throughout this chapter that shape how the public receives information: how a situation is framed and how unfamiliar (or unknown) the situation is—that is, whether or not society has experience with the scenario.

Operational Design (aka Situational Framing)

When America sends weapons and troops overseas to war, will it automatically create panic in society? It depends on how it is framed. To make this point, let's consider a fictional, newly invented teleportation machine capable of sending people anywhere on earth in a second. All you have to do is walk through the doorway, press a button, and that's it. You've arrived. But there's a sign above the door that reads, "This teleporter fails once per day! Of everyone who uses this machine today, one of you will never be seen again." Would you get in the machine?

Most people would not. When teleportation is framed as a lottery, people will focus on the very real chance that their ticket might be called and they are never seen again. But consider that almost everyone reading this book does, in fact, get into a teleportation machine each day—a much deadlier one—called a car. Statistics say that around 100 people die every single day in a motor vehicle accident. But instead of framing it as a death trap just waiting to happen, we get into vehicles that feature lab-tested safety upgrades engineered for protection, and so we think of the accident as something that will happen to someone else. Because of framing, we aren't scared to "teleport" by car despite the fact that the statistics haven't changed a bit.

ACTION STEP #16: Consider situational framing to help identify if society perceives a crisis.

In the example with the make-believe teleporter, we can easily predict that most people won't get in and use it to travel. With the stock market, if something is framed as a threat, we can also easily predict that people will sell and then buy again in the Act of War Market Pattern. In the following case study, we use the Vietnam War to practice recognizing how a crisis is framed in order to measure society's reaction to it.

CASE STUDY   The Vietnam War

> *"In the final analysis, it is their war. They are the ones who have to win it or lose it. We can help them, we can give them equipment, we can send our men out there as advisors, but they have to win it, the people of Vietnam."*
>
> —PRESIDENT JOHN KENNEDY IN A TELEVISED INTERVIEW WITH WALTER CRONKITE ON SEPTEMBER 2, 1963

The longest war in American history, the Vietnam War, heated up stealthily during the second half of the 1960s, yet identifying the war's true starting point has confounded historians. Defining the actual start of the Vietnam War has been such a contentious topic for scholars that there's even argument about what question is the proper way to frame the discussion.

"When did the president of the United States first decide to support South Vietnam?"

"When did America first send troops and military equipment overseas?"

"When did Congress authorize the president to commit resources to combat in Vietnam?"

The Vietnam War involved five different U.S. presidents, and scholars today have accepted a handful of specific dates as the possible start dates for the war. Two of these experts, Dr. John Carland and Dr. Erin Mahan from the Office of the Secretary of Defense, examined four dates as the most likely candidates in a June 17, 2012, paper titled, "When Did the Vietnam War Start for the United States?" We'll examine each of these dates from an investor's point of view, asking the question, "How has this been framed for society?"

When I read Carland and Mahan's paper, I couldn't help but think of the proverbial boiling frog sitting comfortably in a pot of water on the stove. At some point, the stove is lit, but the frog can't tell yet because the water doesn't immediately change temperature. Instead, the pot of water heats up so slowly the frog can't really tell the environment is changing. By the time the water is boiling and the frog is aware of the fire and the danger, it's too late. It's been sitting in the hot water so long it can't jump out, and the frog ends up cooked alive.

Typically, when the government declares war, the people feel immediately and personally affected. But what if it's not framed as a war? Dr. Carland and Dr. Mahan proposed that, before 1950, it was obvious the United States was not engaged in war, and then, after July 28, 1965, it was just as clear the United States was engaged in war. From their point of view, somewhere between these two dates is when the fire was lit and the Vietnam War started.

Situational framing makes the question, "When did the Vietnam War start?" woefully inadequate from an investor's point of view. For us, a better question is, "On what date did the average American feel affected by the government's involvement in the Vietnam War?" As this frog-in-boiling-water tale of the Vietnam War unfolds, we'll stop at the key points to analyze how the crisis was framed and the resulting public reaction.

The empty pot is set on the stove.

In 1954, the first Indochina War had just ended and the Geneva Conference divided Vietnam into Northern and Southern halves. Each was ruled by a completely separate organization, one communist and one democratic, with elections scheduled to reunite the country later under a single government selected by the people. As time passed, North Vietnam's communist leader, Ho Chi Minh, captured the loyalty of the Vietnamese in a way the democratic South Vietnam leader, Ngo Dinh Diem, could not.

The first U.S. president involved with the Vietnam War, Dwight D. Eisenhower, helped create the Southeast Asia Treaty Organization with the purpose of stopping communist influence in Southeast Asia. When it appeared the country might vote to unite under communism, Eisenhower broke the commitments made at the Geneva Convention and began to lay plans for how America could force democracy onto Vietnam. He never could have foreseen a future where more than 8.7 million U.S. troops would serve, and more than 2.3 million would die by the end of the Vietnam War.

In later years, many protestors felt the United States should have kept the bargain struck in Geneva, which required America, and the world, to respect the vote of the Vietnamese people, regardless of outcome. This set the stage for the South Vietnamese communist guerillas, called Viet Cong, and the soldiers from North Vietnam, called Viet Minh, to work together for the unified Vietnam that had been promised them. But, at the time, this was all abstract politics and typical Americans felt no threat from it.

The pot is filled with water.

John F. Kennedy, the second president involved in the Vietnam War, pledged additional aid to the South Vietnam in 1961. Interestingly, just three weeks before Kennedy was assassinated, he'd approved a much different approach to influencing the Vietnamese vote. That original plan involved actively supporting a coup to overthrow Ngo Dinh Diem in the South so a different leader, better suited to U.S. interests, might change the course of the election. It's difficult to imagine today, but if Kennedy hadn't been killed, his administration would likely have orchestrated a coup against a government in South Vietnam, which the United States had originally supported.

In reality, Kennedy's primary role in Vietnam was to further U.S. involvement with advisors, machinery, and the first small commitment of military troops in the second half of 1961. This is the first date historians say could be the start of the war, and a Prepared Investor would have taken notice when President Kennedy signed the National Security Action Memorandum No. 111, dated November 22, 1961. The document stated, "The U.S. Government is prepared to join the Viet-Nam Government in a sharply increased joint effort to avoid a further deterioration in the situation in South Viet-Nam."

But how was this framed? The frog is still unaware of the flame under the pot, because there isn't any. This was not a declaration of war. In fact, it's a clear declaration that the situation was *not* war. It was only a statement of what the country was prepared to do. It didn't say it will happen, and, in direct contradiction, the president consistently framed the overall scenario as "their war." In the end, this was just a memo, and the following analysis of the market's reaction shows the public saw no threat. If society felt America was going to war in a meaningful way, we'd see a very familiar downward movement in the stock market and the following chart (figure 6.1 on facing page) does not show that at all.

With this NSA Memo in place, President Kennedy broke with Eisenhower's limited policy of offering only training, advice, and support. Instead, the United States sent a specially created military unit called the USNS Core to arrive in South Vietnam on December 11, 1961. This is the second date many historians credit as the actual start of the war. The USNS Core consisted of thirty-three H/CH-21 Shawnee/Vertol 44 helicopters and four hundred crewmen to operate and maintain them. Less than two weeks later, the helicopters were providing combat support in an operation near Saigon. Allowing the helicopters to support South Vietnamese combat operations meant American pilots were ferrying troops to and from the field as well as providing fire support and training for South Vietnamese operations.

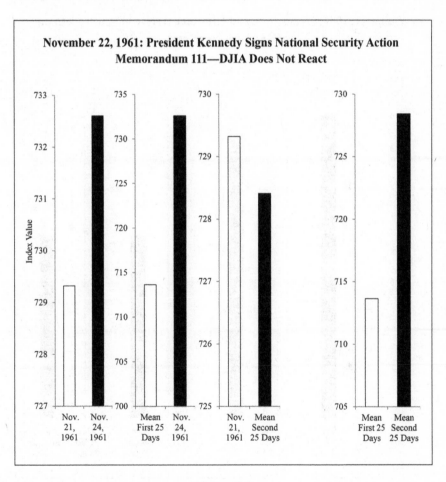

Figure 6.1

At the time, a Prepared Investor could not have ignored the United States getting involved like that because part of being prepared requires attention to events that could be considered an overt act of war. But if society felt it was a meaningful crisis, the following chart (figure 6.2 below) would have shown the general market dropping definitively right after the catalyst occurred. But for both the NSA Memo and the sending of troops and equipment, the market doesn't act that way at all.

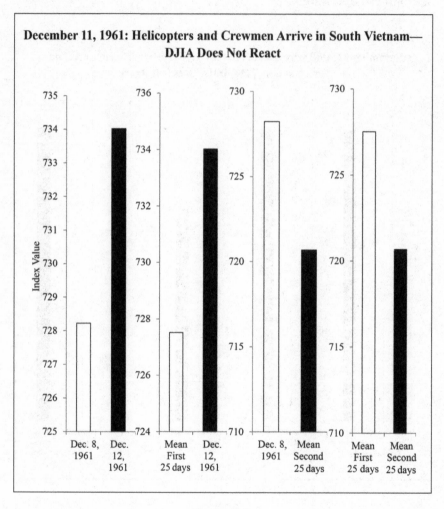

Figure 6.2

As those helicopters left the United States, President Kennedy took the first steps toward a new and improved war machine that would change the concept of modern warfare. The "Huey" helicopter became a type of airborne bus system carrying American GIs with notes and photos folded under the bands around their helmets. The B-52 Stratofortress, designed to drop bombs from a high altitude on long-range missions, ultimately flew tens of thousands of bombing flights in North and South Vietnam, Cambodia, and Laos. Also in the sky, the F-4 Phantom fighter plane, armed with a 20-millimeter cannon and air-to-air missiles, served as a fast, maneuverable bomber delivering conventional or radar-guided payloads to enemy targets. On the ground, the M113 armored personnel carrier carried between 12 and 38 millimeters of protective armor and had a .50 caliber browning machine gun along with two optional M60 machine guns. The carrier could contain up to eleven soldiers and travel securely in amphibious environments, making it perfect for the Vietnamese terrain.

But on the date the first thirty-three helicopters arrived, the full extent of the war machine was still hidden from view. Many scholars today select this date as the start of the Vietnam War because they have the benefit of hindsight. However, in that moment, neither America nor the stock market reacted to a crisis because it simply wasn't framed as one.

Situational framing trumps historical data when examining world events from an investor's point of view. Americans trusted their televised and print news reports about that initial arrival carrying only a single shipment of 400 people. The implication was "This isn't a crisis, it's a shipment. It's a package. It's a single, special military unit going to assist a small country on the other side of the globe." The textbook fact that troops were going to Vietnam for the purpose of war was only an empty pot getting filled with water.

147

The flame beneath the pot is lit.

After the assassination of President John F. Kennedy, Lyndon B. Johnson was quickly sworn in and became immediately involved in the Vietnam War. Despite passing more than sixty education bills, the Civil Rights Act of 1968, and sending three American astronauts to successfully orbit the moon, historians have defined Johnson's presidency by the war in Vietnam. LBJ, however, tried to define things differently. At Akron University on October 21, 1964, President Johnson announced, "We are not about to send American boys nine or ten thousand miles away from home to do what Asian boys ought to be doing for themselves."

He said this because, two months earlier, he'd approached Congress asking permission to increase military presence in Vietnam after two U.S. destroyers reported they'd been attacked by North Vietnamese forces. Congress approved Johnson's request on August 7, 1964, by passing the Gulf of Tonkin Resolution, which authorized the president to take any measures he believed necessary to retaliate. This resolution became the legal basis for Johnson, and later Nixon, to wage war in Vietnam. For that reason, many say this was the actual start of the Vietnam War, though doubts later emerged about whether the American destroyers in the Gulf of Tonkin had truly been attacked in the first place. The following chart (figure 6.3 on facing page) demonstrates an ambivalent investing public who did not see a material threat deserving any meaningful reaction.

It didn't take long before LBJ used the authority granted by the Gulf of Tonkin Resolution to wage the Vietnam War characterized by movies and books today. Expecting North Vietnam to weaken when faced with more frequent bombing raids, President Johnson ordered the launch of Operation Rolling Thunder, a bombing campaign that lasted more than two years. At the onset of Operation Rolling Thunder, the president held a midday press conference to announce the U.S. goals for involvement in Vietnam. Questioned by the press, President Johnson spoke about the effects the conflict had on the U.S. economy and discussed the possibility of hostilities escalating into a larger war. America heard Johnson's address from a perspective

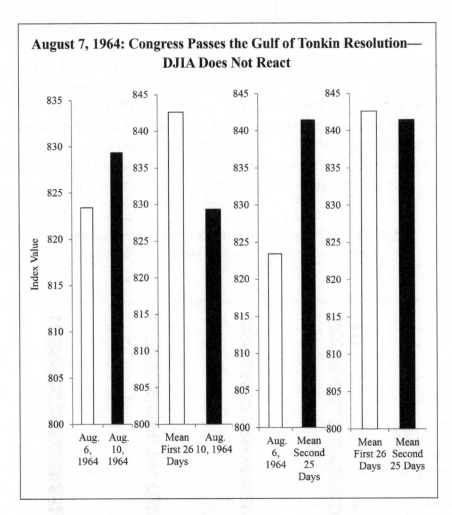

Figure 6.3

that is difficult to conjure in today's more cynical and jaded society. People in 1965 still pined for the recently canceled *Leave It To Beaver* sitcom and believed in Norman Rockwell's "Officer Friendly," pictured on covers of the *Saturday Evening Post*. Most of America left their doors unlocked saying, "What if someone needed to get in?"

Instead of a major crisis, they heard about an ongoing operation called Rolling Thunder. Instead of an active enemy, they heard about how to "construct a clear definition of America's role in the

Vietnam conflict." Instead of a threat to their lives, Americans heard about "limits of our national objectives" and "the constant effort on our part to bring this . . . to a quick and honorable end." When the president explained how hostilities may later escalate into a large-scale war, he was also hinting that the crisis was still to come because the country was not yet at war. While he reiterated his commitment to negotiate with the Viet Cong at "any time, any place," the New York Stock Exchange remained open until normal closing time, and the next chart (figure 6.4 below) shows the lack of reaction.

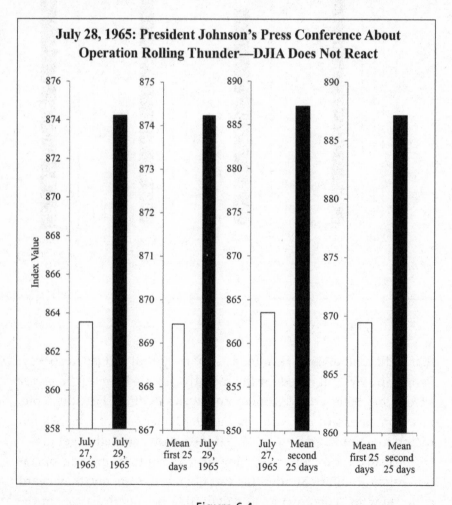

Figure 6.4

The pot begins to boil.

In late January 1968, during the Lunar New Year also known as Tet, North Vietnamese troops and communist Viet Cong guerrillas launched a coordinated attack against South Vietnam. At the end of the Tet Offensive, both sides had suffered losses, and, oddly enough, both sides claimed victory. On March 31, 1968, Johnson announced he would not seek a second term as president, which meant the job of finding a way out of Vietnam was left to his successor, Richard M. Nixon, who would also prove not up to the task. Six months after taking office, President Nixon announced, "The United States is going to encourage, and has a right to expect, that this problem will be increasingly handled by, and the responsibility for it taken by, the Asian nations themselves." Although that message is essentially the same operational design as Nixon's predecessors, this framework became known as the Nixon Doctrine.

Nixon waged the war for two more years with his "personal assurances . . . that the United States will react very strongly and rapidly to any violation. . . ." This suggested that a major reaction still had not happened. Many felt Nixon meant to bring back the B-52s and their extensive bombing campaigns, but in the end, the Watergate scandal took over all his attention and Vice President Gerald R. Ford took office. As president, Ford declared the Vietnam War ended on April 23, 1975. Seven days later, North Vietnamese tanks rolled through the gates of the presidential palace in Saigon, and South Vietnam "fell" to the communist regime they would have voted for from the start.

Did the public ever react, from an investor's point of view, to the Vietnam War?

Nixon could not have accomplished nearly five years of military escalation nor engaged in so much additional conflict in Vietnam had it not been for the draft. Originally, the draft was framed as something that would happen to someone else. An individual's age was the determining factor in the draft, and it was easy to understand where you were in the lineup. *It's not even our war, right? There aren't that many people going anyway.* It was easy to believe that someone else would end up going to Vietnam because, systemically, it was framed as someone else's problem.

That suddenly changed when the draft became a national lottery on December 1, 1969. On that day, the entire fighting-age population of the United States might "win" a ticket to go to war. Held at the Selective Service National Headquarters in Washington, DC, the lottery determined the order of who would be called for duty during the calendar year 1970.

A lottery is a powerful framework because somebody has to win, and people cannot help but think it might be them. This is how modern-day lottery tickets keep getting sold all over America, despite the overwhelming odds against ever winning anything. In December 1969, the destiny of many sons, brothers, and fathers was contained in a large glass basin where a jumble of 366 blue plastic capsules offered everyone a chance to "win" draft orders. Drawn by hand, the blue capsule had a date that assigned the order of call to all men within the eighteen to twenty-six age range. Officials hoped the lottery would add an element of surprise to the process and mitigate the problem of draft dodgers. Each with their own contentious, multisided story for why they didn't go to war, famous draft dodgers of the Vietnam era include Dick Cheney, Bill Clinton, Donald Trump, and Muhammad Ali.

Before the lottery occurred, people felt someone else would have to go because the system framed it that way. But when the lottery went into effect, society as a whole abruptly felt they could be selected to go and worried about "winning" just as much as today's lotto players hope to win a jackpot prize. The December 1, 1969, lottery isn't typically recognized by scholars as "the start of the Vietnam war" because, logically, it certainly isn't. But it is the point when the average American felt affected. It is the date the crisis became personal to everyone in the United States, and framing had everything to do with it. The stock market's reaction should look familiar (figure 6.5 on facing page).

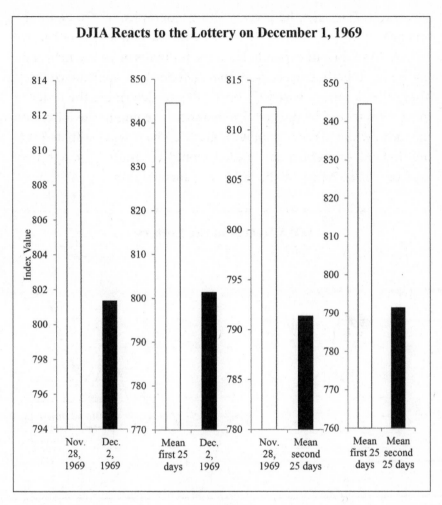

Figure 6.5

How long does it take for investors to get comfortable with this new draft phenomenon? The following chart (figure 6.6 on the following page) shows, just as in past crisis scenarios, the cloud passes swiftly.

The lottery, like most crises, had such an impact that you can see its shadow stretch across much of modern memory of those years. One of the richest men in the world, Ray Dalio, published a book in 2017 about his approach to business structure and organizational success. In *Principles*, he gives a short biography where he briefly touches on how he dodged the draft with the help of his father. He writes, "As the draft expanded and the numbers of young men coming home in body bags soared, the Vietnam War split the country. There was a lottery based on birthdates to determine the order of those who would be drafted. I remember listening to the lottery on the radio while playing pool with my friends. It was estimated that the first 160 or so birthdays called would be drafted, though they read off all 366 dates. My birthday was forty-eighth."

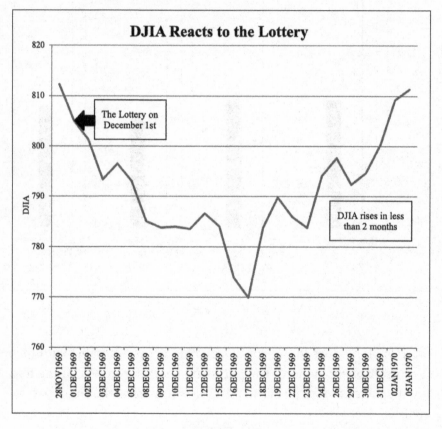

Figure 6.6

Dalio remembers where he was at the moment of the lottery almost fifty years ago. He remembers the actual number he was assigned. He's not alone in this. The country viewed the new system as a crisis because it was framed that way.

Rush Limbaugh experienced a similar situation after he dropped out of Southeast Missouri State University, causing him to lose his student deferment. Selective Service records suggest his private doctor, instead of an armed forces physician, gave a medical opinion that Limbaugh was disqualified for service by a nearly meaningless condition called a pilonidal cyst. Because Limbaugh broadcasts from a conservative, patriotic platform, many fans and critics alike expressed that he did not have a legitimate reason to avoid serving since the malady could be easily corrected by a minor surgery. Ever the performer, Limbaugh kept the controversy afloat by occasionally goading callers into entertaining conversations about it. But the one time he discussed his service to the nation with some seriousness with ABC newsman Jeff Greenfield, he, like Dalio, highlighted the lottery as a meaningful event in the timeline. He said, "I had student deferments in college and, upon taking a physical, was discovered to have a . . . physical deferment and then the lottery system came along . . ."

I don't expect historians to suddenly change their mind and declare the lottery the start of the Vietnam War. But I do think investors who want to be prepared for crisis need to accept that keeping up with current events is only half the challenge. You also have to understand how situational framing will change what society sees, how they will react, and what they will remember. For example, Nixon established the policy of Détente with the Soviet Union, laid the foundation for the Middle East peace process, launched the war on cancer, and helped start a peaceful desegregation of public schools in the south. But how is he remembered? His legacy crumbled into the Watergate scandal (which readers will recognize as a leader-driven threat to which the stock market reacted predictably).

If we go only by the textbooks and refuse to let framing influence us, Nixon's memory should evoke images of the most communist dictator with anti-American values that the country has ever had. It's hard to believe, but President Nixon successfully imposed two separate economic freezes on both wages and prices in a draconian power grab that rings of old-world Russia. How could it be just a little footnote in history that an American president wrested the power of money from the public's hands and took control of nearly everything from workers' salaries to apartment rents on two separate occasions? The question isn't just about what happened, it's about operational design. Though the economic freezes were like something out of Ayn Rand's *Atlas Shrugged*, it was framed as "the cure for difficult times," and, ultimately, the moves were popular with the majority of Americans. Situational framing changes everything.

Known versus Unknown

There's a nice waterpark near my home, and the first time my family went, one of my daughters was frightened to go down the slides. It didn't matter how well the situation was framed with friendly decorations and signs explaining how to ride the waterslides safely. For her, it was a new experience—it was the unknown—and she was very scared. When she finally did take the plunge after hours of cajoling, she found it enjoyable and was the loudest to complain when it was time to leave that day. Having experience is another way of saying "I'm used to it."

Imagine a young, newlywed couple who decide to move into a Chicago apartment right above the city's elevated metro system. Every time the "L" rumbles by, they hear it. But not for long because, with experience, they get used to it. Over time, the train's noise doesn't make an impact on them like it did back when the sound was unfamiliar to them.

While enjoying a typical Friday, one of them sees a Tweet about . . . *wait, a war in Ohio?* On Facebook, they learn that United States soldiers have mobilized and are attacking and killing fellow Americans hundreds of miles away from them. They've never seen this before and get swept up in the ranting, emotional comments on social media. *This is unprecedented! The government is killing its own citizens! It's a crisis!* A seed of fear blossoms, fed by TV news, Twitter feeds, and neighbors talking about civil war and martial law. The fear quickly grows into a "fight or flight" need to take action as they see their community suddenly making mass withdrawals from banks and loading up at grocery stores. *I better sell my investments before I lose everything!*

People panic and sell their investments with particular zeal when a perceived threat is coupled with the fear of the unknown. Adrenaline is a funny thing. Produced in the oldest part of our brain, the medulla oblongata, it's the hormone that influences our fight-or-flight response and protects us from the dangers we perceive in the moment. But after the adrenaline dissipates, oftentimes we are left with the fallout from the realization that we did not act in our own best interest.

For this hypothetical Chicago couple, the negative energy and fake news fueled emotions for a short period of time. The unknown felt like a logical reason to sell everything and "get out" before the stocks, the banks, and the whole world would go bust. Afterwards, they don't feel scared anymore because the threats and the social media turmoil have subsided, and they can see things differently. The problem, of course, is that they cannot undo their actions made in the heat of the moment.

ACTION STEP #17: Use social experience to help read the room and identify if society perceives a crisis.

Without experience, education, and training to guide their actions, people are highly unlikely to make good choices in the face of an unknown threat. This emotional, ill-advised conduct is not rare. When it occurs on a large scale without an actual threat involved, it's labeled mass hysteria. The American Psychological Association defines "mass hysteria" as "the spontaneous outbreak of atypical thoughts, feelings, or actions in a group or social aggregate. Manifestations may include…bizarre actions…epidemic manias and panics, such as…radio listeners' reactions to the Orson Welles broadcast based on H. G. Wells's War of the Worlds in 1938. Also called group hysteria; epidemic hysteria; and collective hysteria."

When President John F. Kennedy was shot in Texas, what illusion of threat convinced investors in Seattle to sell their stocks? Did any seller honestly believe that publicly traded companies were suddenly going to have fewer customers for their products? Yet, as we know, the stock market plunged a day after his assassination. This irrational, and predictable, response is not labeled mass hysteria simply because the president really was killed.

It's not challenging to recognize an actual threat from a terrorist or an overt act of war, but it's another skill altogether to assess how society understands it. A Prepared Investor must identify when something that might not be truly threatening, but because it is unknown to society, is *perceived* as a threat. The next case study uses the shooting at Kent State to highlight how society's level of experience can help a Prepared Investor identify the spark for the next crisis.

CASE STUDY The Kent State Shooting

"The one thing every man fears is the unknown."
—HENRY A. KISSINGER

From the end of the 1960s, the Dow Jones Industrial Average continued to rise until it finally reached the 1,000-point milestone on November 14, 1972. Cheers were heard on the floor of the New York Stock Exchange. People remember 1972 as the year *The Godfather* was in theaters and Americans watched *All in the Family* on television. Investors enjoyed the "nifty-fifty stocks," which was a list of popular large-cap companies people called "one decision stocks" because they could buy them and, since they were so secure, never worry about selling. Among the nifty-fifty were companies such as IBM and McDonald's. The Dow Jones Industrial Average reaching 1,000 was a powerful psychological milestone after the country had watched the index repeatedly flirt with that mark for years, but never attain it.

However, there was a very interesting dip in the stock market on its way to the 1,000-point milestone. This downswing occurred after America experienced a tragedy it had never imagined, and people reacted to the crisis like any other collective catastrophic threat. The Kent State shooting resulted in death, caused millions of students to strike, closed schools all over the country, and gave rise to an unforgettable Crosby, Stills & Nash song.

In today's world, killer clowns, zombie apocalypses, and end-of-the-universe Mayan prophecies are an everyday cultural staple delivered to us nearly every hour by our cell phones and the internet. Almost every American has been exposed to dystopian stories about a government that lies and kills its own citizens. But back in 1970, not only did it happen, the nation was completely unprepared for it. On May 4, when the Ohio National Guard opened fire and killed four students and wounded nine others on the campus of Kent State University, the United States lost an important part of its innocence. Photos depicting military troops in formation with Humvees and M16s rang out like an act of war to an inexperienced society. These photographs were so powerful that one of them, taken by twenty-two-year-old John Paul Filo, earned a Pulitzer Prize.

To say America, at this point, was against the war in Vietnam is an understatement. Thousands of people were upending their lives to march in protest. When President Nixon announced on April 30, 1970, that American troops would join the South Vietnamese People's Army to invade Cambodia and disrupt North Vietnamese supply lines, there was backlash all across the country. At a small private school in Ohio, Nixon's televised announcement led to a gathering of students who wished to voice their disagreement with the policy.

Newsweek's coverage of the Kent State shooting, headlined, "My God! They're Killing Us" is an iconic description of what transpired to create the unfathomable situation where youths wishing to express their opinions were considered threatening enough to warrant a military response. It's difficult to imagine the shock of these young adults when they realized their own countrymen were shooting at them. By the time it was over, much had happened that couldn't be undone.

While it's easy to find articles about the Kent State shooting itself, it's much more difficult to find the *Wall Street Journal's* description of the stock market published the day after the tragedy: "Stock prices took their steepest dive since President Kennedy's assassination on Nov. 22 1963, and the Dow Jones industrial average plunged [to] . . . its lowest level since that day." (Figures 6.7 and 6.8)

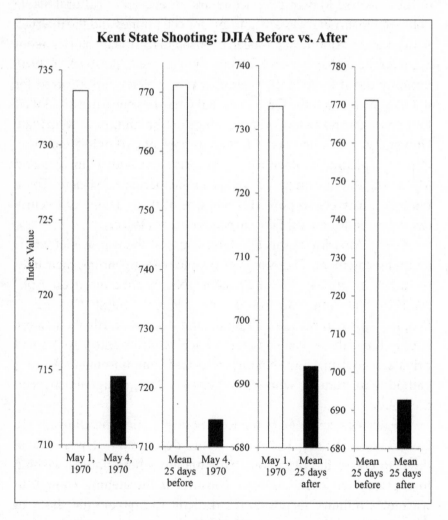

Figure 6.7

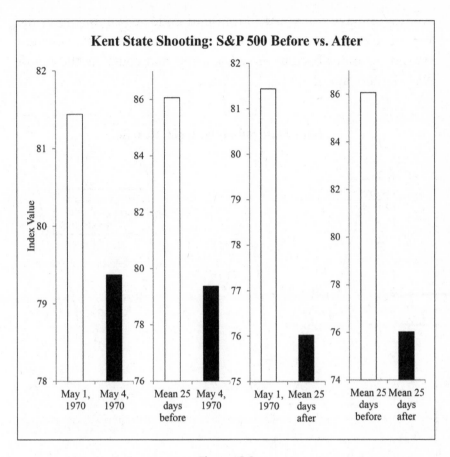

Figure 6.8

The two previous charts (figures 6.7 and 6.8) show the characteristic drop forming the first part of the Act of War Market Pattern. The following charts (figures 6.9 and 6.10 on the following pages) show the pattern in its entirety demonstrating that this new, unknown situation immediately sparked fear for investors. It's obvious to us today that publicly traded companies weren't going out of business due to this tragic episode. People all over the United States would still gas up their cars, eat cereal, and go to work the following week despite the fact that four students lost their lives. Nevertheless, investors sold their investments and drove down the market. What's more, these charts show that, even though millions of students all over the country continued to refuse to go to school long after the Kent State shooting, the investing public quickly reinvested enough to send the index back to pre-crisis levels and complete the Act of War Market Pattern.

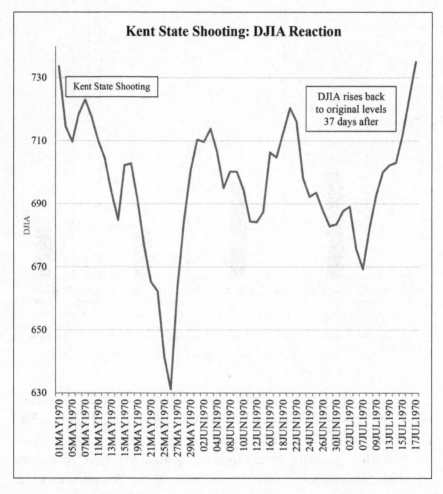

Figure 6.9—Kent State Shooting, DJIA rises back to original levels 37 days after shooting

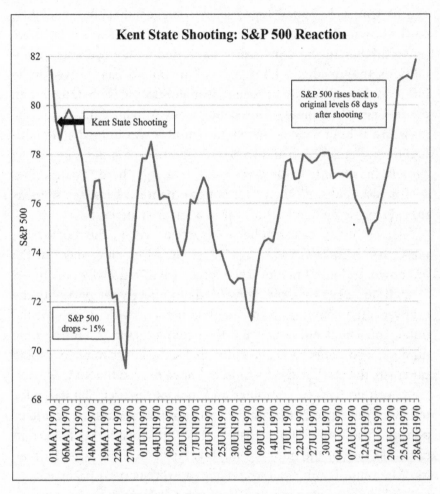

Figure 6.10—S&P 500 drops ~ 15%, S&P 500 rises
back to original levels 68 days after shooting

This massacre, as it was called at the time, certainly was not the start of actual combat or civil war or *The Hunger Games*. But it was an unknown. Society had no experience with this kind of event. It was more than just a surprise—it was *new*.

What illusion of threat occurred across the country to cause so many people to sell their stocks after the Kent State shooting? Andrew Lo, who studies emotions and economics at the Massachusetts Institute of Technology told CBS News, "The research that neuroscientists have developed seem to suggest that herd mentality, on the downside - that is, in reaction to panic and fear - is far more powerful than the herd mentality associated with greed - herd mentality on the upside..." Lo suggests humankind has evolved to be influenced more greatly by feeling fear and fleeing from danger than the feeling of happiness caused by an investment gain. When the massacre at Kent State occurred, the country was immediately notified through television and radio. *The government is attacking its own citizens!* In response to the perceived threat, this "herd" Lo describes sold investments and then later bought them back just the same as they'd react to an overt act of war or a terrorist attack.

Almost every catastrophe we've gone over in this book from the Cuban Missile Crisis to 9/11 has offered us an element of the unknown. It doesn't matter if the disaster will rationally only affect a small number of people. For a crisis to affect your portfolio, the catalyst often combines a threatening element with a sense of the unknown. The deadliness is not the driving factor. If ten times the number of students had been killed that same afternoon in a terrible car crash, the stock market would not have moved the same way.

If you go to your computer and look at the S&P 500 index for the month of April 2013, you'll clearly see that something bad happened. There's an obvious U-shaped Act of War Market Pattern in the latter half of the month. Monday, April 15, 2013, was the Boston Marathon bombing. Two teenage terrorists used backpacks to smuggle into the race multiple bombs made from pressure cookers. There are places in the world where this very localized damage from two small-range, handmade bombs would hardly be news. But this delivery method and the vulnerability of the public gathering for the race was new and unique to America. Society had no experience with this unknown and, therefore, reacted predictably.

Contrast that tragedy with the market movement of the S&P 500 in April and May 1999. The Columbine High School shooting occurred on April 20, 1999, and there's no doubt it was a crisis and a travesty. But years before, an engineering student had shot and killed fifteen people on the University of Texas campus in Austin.

On the Kent State campus years earlier, the very authorities designed to protect Americans had also killed students. Columbine's tragedy cannot be overstated. It was a horror that should never have happened. But for investors, where the unknown is an important factor, it wasn't as scary because it wasn't new. Like the couple living in Chicago by the "L," investors only hear the train when they are still new to the sound. If the public is used to the noise, they simply cannot hear it as well.

With this in mind, what can a Prepared Investor do when the next unknown threat occurs? The next case study provides a hypothetical example of how John Miller, a college professor from Maryland, manages his portfolio in reaction to the Kent State shooting. In the previous chapter, you read about how Sally Smith reacted to 9/11 and the importance of knowing your own risk parameters. John Miller decides to take a little more risk than Sally did, and the contrast between the two might be helpful when making decisions for your own approach in the future.

Prepared Investor Profile: John Miller and His Portfolio Actions after the Kent State Shooting

"Prepare for the unknown by studying how others in the past have coped with the unforeseeable and the unpredictable."
—GENERAL GEORGE S. PATTON

An experienced investor, John Miller, has two investment accounts totaling $1 million, which he actively manages with an advisory team. He has a close friend named Greg who just recently retired. The two men occasionally golf together and share personal financial information with one another. John is just as comfortable betting the market will drop as he is betting on the market advancing. He often works with his professional financial advisor to sell short and buy long to profit from those market movements. He used to use options regularly, but when his friend Greg stopped using options at retirement, John decided to stop as well. John's $1 million is currently all invested in various stocks, bonds, mutual funds, and exchange traded funds, and he has no short positions. The portfolio has margin capability, which he uses occasionally as a tool to amplify his return.

After reading this book, John and his advisor laid plans for how they'd react when the next unknown threat occurred. As it happens, John never spoke about this with Greg. The following timeline demonstrates how John Miller might have behaved using today's tools and technologies on the backdrop of the real dates and market values surrounding the Kent State shooting. This hypothetical example begins on May 4, 1970, when Mr. Miller, the college professor, heads to work at the University of Maryland.

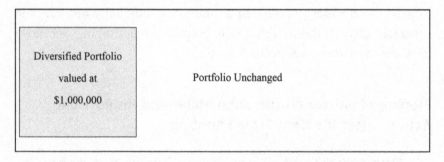

Figure A. Portfolio Unchanged Before Kent State Shooting

Midday that Monday, John sees the shooting on Facebook and reads a lot of Twitter chatter related to it. Immediately, he calls his financial advisor to short the market because the event met all the criteria for a new threat for which society had no experience. John wanted to meaningfully and decisively act as soon as he could after it happened. He understood this was extremely risky because he couldn't be sure his assessment of the public's reaction was accurate, but it was a risk he accepted.

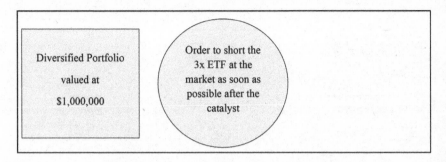

Figure B. Place Order to Short Sell ETF

John's advisor sells $300,000 worth of an ETF that tracks the S&P 500 with three times the return. The market had already moved down a bit when the order goes through.

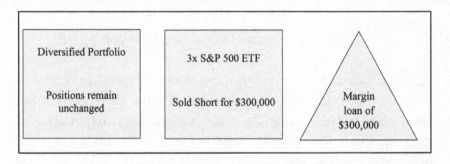

Figure C. Owns a Short Position

John's financial advisor sees the pre-event value for the S&P 500 index was 709, and she calculates a 7 percent drop from the pre-crisis close to be 660. With John's approval, she prepares to buy and cover the short position so that it will happen when the S&P 500 hits 660.

167

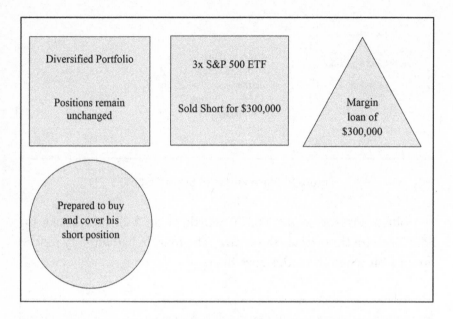

Figure D. Prepared to Cover Short Position

That same day, John and his financial advisor calculate that this first trade will create a profit of more than $60,000. But because of not executing the trade immediately, imperfect ETF tracking, margin cost, and transaction fees, they plan for a profit of $54,000. Additionally, they prepare to buy $354,000 of the same long 3x S&P 500 ETF when the index hits 660. Lastly, they plan to sell the entire long position costing $354,000 when the index has risen back to 706.

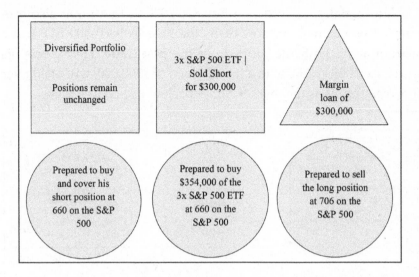

Figure E. Prepared for Final Trades

As the market drops in reaction to the shooting, John's order to buy and cover his short position goes through by May 26, 1970. He doesn't capture profit for the full 7 percent drop because he was a little late getting involved. Still, he earned the $54,000 they were expecting.

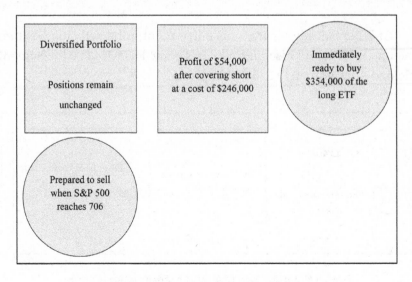

Figure F. Short Trade Is Closed Out

Additionally, his order to buy $354,000 at that point also executes. This means John now owns the long 3x S&P 500 ETF using margin along with the profit from the first trade. He expects his purchase of $354,000, with a margin loan of $300,000, will yield over 7 percent profit as the market comes back to pre-crisis levels.

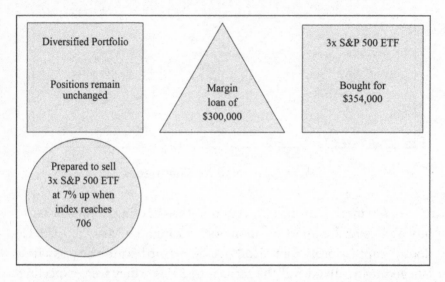

Figure G. Order to Buy Executes and Margin Loan Is Extended

At 7 percent higher than his entry point, John sells his position by June 1, 1970, and his margin loan is gone. His $354,000 investment yielded approximately $75,000 in profit.

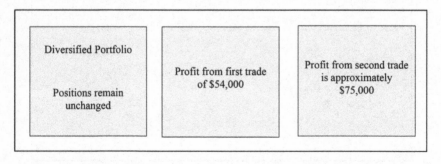

Figure H. Order Executes and Margin Loan Is Gone

In July of that year, John Miller looks over his May and June investment statements and confirms everything happened the way he wanted it to. The first trade shorting the market yielded about $54,000 in profit, and the second trade betting on the market rising earned him over $75,000. His traditional, well-diversified portfolio was untouched throughout, and, for the $1 million portfolio overall, he earned about $130,000 in profit that could help cushion any future blows to his return. While he knows that's a profit of over 100 percent on an annualized basis, he tends to think in simpler terms and is glad the entire process yielded a portfolio return of a little less than 13 percent in about one month. The next chart shows the entire picture.

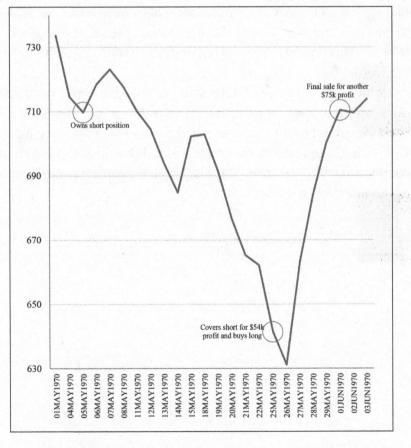

Figure I: John Miller's Response to the Kent State Shooting

The next time John and his friend are golfing, Greg admits that he'd sold some positions in late May. When John doesn't reply, Greg exclaims, "Come on, have you ever seen a situation like that? It's unprecedented! I mean, what's next, we lose all our civil liberties? It's definitely going to get worse, John. I'm glad I went to cash."

But by selling, Greg has two serious problems. First, he altered his portfolio so it might not be aligned to serve his needs anymore. For example, if he needed income from those investments he sold, where will he get that income now? Second, he has to decide when to buy back in with the cash he raised. If he does what most people do, he'll wait to buy after plenty of good news helps him feel comfortable that the crisis has passed and a purchase is finally warranted. In that typical scenario, Greg would have sold low in a fearful reaction to the crisis and then bought those investments back at a higher cost later on. This typical reaction to crisis destroys portfolios and lowers net worth.

John Miller and Sally Smith made moves that could have been done similarly after many of the crises in this book. The following chart (figure 6.11 on the facing page) shows a similar story for the Gulf War. Change the dates and actual index values and the charts continue to look surprisingly similar because people repeatedly react to certain crises in the same way.

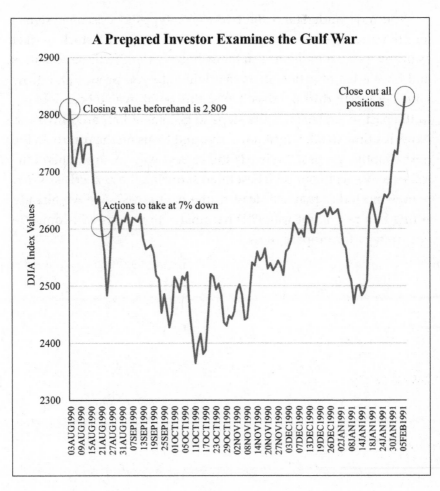

Figure 6.11

You now understand the two major types of crises—systemic and threatening—and the patterns they create in the stock market as investors react to them. You know how to identify these scenarios and have a list of action steps that will help you protect and grow your net worth during crisis. Up to this point, we've been looking to the past to understand the steps to become a Prepared Investor. Now, it's time to take this knowledge and focus on the future. In the next chapter, we ask, "What is the easiest way to strengthen ourselves so we act in our own best interest during the next crisis? What is brewing today that will lead to the next crisis? Are we already sitting in a pot of hot water? What final action steps will complete our strategy for preparedness?"

CHAPTER SEVEN

Cause and Effect, Action and Reaction
How to Use Our Natural Tendencies to Your Advantage

Stanley Milgram, a social psychologist at Yale, conducted a series of now-famous experiments that made the news and contributed an important piece of wisdom for every Prepared Investor: that a third party can greatly influence us. A New York City native, Milgram started his graduate studies in the social relations department at Harvard University in 1954. There, Milgram received instruction from leading social psychologists of the day, including Jerome Bruner, Roger Brown, and Solomon Asch. Milgram was fascinated with Asch's conformity experiments, showing how individual behavior can be influenced by group behavior because individuals often conform to a group's norms, despite the morality or value of that group's choices.

After earning a PhD from Harvard, Milgram accepted a position as an assistant professor at Yale University in 1960. As part of his research, he was intrigued that almost everyone accused at the Nuremberg War Criminal trials for acts of genocide defended themselves by saying that they were only following orders from their superiors. A year after the Jerusalem-based trial of Nazi leader, Adolf Eichmann, Milgram had devised an experiment he thought would answer some basic questions. Could it be that Eichmann and people like him in the Holocaust were just following orders? Is it appropriate to view men like Eichmann differently than we would the rest of society? How far would the typical person go in obeying an instruction that obviously harms somebody else? Can ordinary people be easily influenced to commit atrocities? Do people consistently do something they normally wouldn't when faced with the proper catalyst situation?

Milgram advertised in the newspaper to get his volunteers and paid them $4.50 each for showing up. At the beginning of each encounter, an actor dressed in a scientist's lab coat would introduce the volunteer to another participant as if they both were there in the same capacity. But this other person was secretly a second actor helping Milgram's with the experiment. The Experimenter in the lab coat told the volunteer and masquerading staff member to draw straws to determine which job they would get: either a Learner or a Teacher. The straws, however, were not random, meaning the staff member was always the Learner and each volunteer believed he was selected as Teacher by chance.

The experiment took up two rooms in the Yale Interaction Laboratory, and the Learner-staff-member was seated in a fake electric chair in one room, while in the other, the Teacher-volunteer and Experimenter-actor had a convincing-looking electric shock generator. The Teacher-volunteer could not see the Learner-staff-member on the other side of the wall. The Teacher's job was to help the Learner get familiar with a list of word pairs by talking through an intercom, and afterward, the Teacher would test the Learner by naming a word and wait for the Learner to recall its pair from a list of four possible choices. This setup has inspired many other experiments and entered popular culture through books, songs, and movies (like the opening scene of *Ghostbusters*).

In his role as Teacher, the volunteer understood he must administer an electric shock every time the Learner made a mistake. To add to the drama, the volunteer was required to increase the level of shock each time. Though there was no actual electrical shock, the Teacher sat at a realistic contraption with thirty switches marked from fifteen volts labeled as a "slight shock" to 450 volts labeled as,

"Danger—severe shock." The Learner gave mainly wrong answers on purpose, and for each of these, the unsuspecting Teacher gave him what appeared to be an electric shock. If the innocent Teacher refused to administer a shock or said anything to question the planned series of events, the actor in the lab coat (the Experimenter) gave a specific series of orders to prompt the volunteer to continue. Here are the four exact statements the Experimenter would say and only in this order:

PROD 1: Please continue.

PROD 2: The experiment requires you to continue.

PROD 3: It is absolutely essential that you continue.

PROD 4: You have no other choice but to continue.

Here follows an example of what the volunteer would hear upon triggering the supposedly painful shocks at the higher levels:

90 volts: "Ugh!"

105 volts: "Ugh!" (Louder)

120 volts: "Ugh! Hey, this really hurts."

150 volts: "Ugh! Experimenter! That's all. Get me out of here. I told you I had heart trouble. My heart's starting to bother me now. Get me out of here, please. My heart's starting to bother me. I refuse to go on. Let me out."

As the Learner on the other side of the wall gets questions wrong on purpose, the Teacher delivers a shock and hears persuasive indications of pain and suffering. When I read this the first time, I thought that the 150-volt level would be the point where I would have stopped if I was the Teacher in the experiment. I wonder how many readers feel the same way. To prepare for the experiment, Milgram wrote the Learner's script quite a bit longer.

165 volts: (Shouting) "Ugh! Let me out!"

180 volts: (Shouting) "Ugh! I can't stand the pain. Let me out of here!"

195 volts: "Ugh! Let me out of here. Let me out of here. My heart's bothering me. Let me out of here! You have no right to keep me here! Let me out! Let me out of here! Let me out! Let me out of here! My heart's bothering me. Let me out! Let me out!"

210 volts: "Ugh! Experimenter! Get me out of here. I've had enough. I won't be in the experiment anymore."

Most people would have a hard time connecting to what it must be like to hear this in real life. But try to imagine a convincing actor on the other side of a wall saying fearfully that their heart is bothering them. He is shouting and begging to "get me out of here." Imagine the Teacher-volunteer who, after 195 volts, just picks up another card, hears a wrong answer, and hits the 210-volt shock. The experiment continues and, four separate shocks later, the Teacher is at 270 volts, and the Learner starts screaming almost incoherently to be released. Four more shocks after that, and the voltage is at 330. This is when the Learner cries out for the last time that his heart is bothering him. The next five individual shocks go all the way to 450 volts, and the Teacher hears only silence. For those last questions, the Teacher would continue to shock the learner because a silent response is a wrong answer. The ominous silence coming from the Learner's side was meant to be interpreted as incapacitation or even death. Milgram and the actors didn't think anyone was actually going to get to this point, but that was the script outlining what they were prepared to do.

The results of the experiment were astonishing to everyone. In the end, the majority of Teacher-volunteers continued to the highest level of 450 volts despite all the signs they were harming, perhaps killing, the person on the other side of the wall. The experiment was often terminated by the Experimenter because the script was complete, and there was nothing else to do. Additionally, *every single participant continued to 300 volts*, meaning every Teacher-volunteer went past that 150-volt level and seriously hurt the Learner in the other room. Milgram carried out eighteen variations of this study and effectively concluded that ordinary people are highly likely to follow orders given by an authority figure. People follow these orders despite their morality or values.

With a certain catalyst, people who aren't prepared are extremely predictable. This is why, if every traffic light turned green at an intersection at once, there would be a car accident. It's also why, when a crisis lines up as I've described in this book, investors sell their investments without regard to the details. Whether jettisoning a good company or shocking an innocent human being, given the right environment, the vast majority of people press the button.

▍ ACTION STEP #18: Find a coach.

In his article "The Perils of Obedience," Milgram wrote "The extreme willingness of adults to go to almost any lengths on the command of an authority constitutes the chief finding of the study and the fact most urgently demanding explanation." This is why the coaching profession exists both in the athletic and business world. It's what explains how an Olympic athlete, arguably the best at their particular sport in the entire world, would actually take instruction from somebody else who cannot possibly perform at the same elite level.

When crisis strikes, most investors are likely to do one of two things: trade at inopportune times, or put their head in the sand and do nothing at all. If you designate a coach, some kind of authority that you respect, to help guide you during this time, it greatly increases the odds that you'll react differently. Milgram's experiment helped prove that our natural response is to do what is suggested by an authority in which we believe. So pick an authority figure who will ask you to do things that benefit you and help you achieve your goals.

A professional financial advisor certainly invests for her clients, but when the engagement is operating at its best, the client receives guidance and coaching far beyond the dollars and cents in gain/loss reports. But your guide does not have to be a professional financial advisor. If we're predisposed to do what someone in charge says, then it could be anyone as long as you feel they are sincerely an authority figure. You could lean on a pastor, a parent, a teacher, or any mentor you trust. I suggest you look for that person you know you'll listen to when they need to tell you something you don't wish to hear.

There are successful people who take this so seriously, they've surrounded themselves with a "board of advisors." This is a specific group of trustworthy professionals the successful person deems to have different, complementing expertise. Some individuals won't make any major life decisions without consulting their board of advisors. If you've ever seen the retired basketball player, Shaquille O'Neal, on television, you've seen an extremely successful American who believes in this philosophy and has relied on his board of advisors the majority of his life.

Milgram's findings were appalling to the world and are still a controversial definition of human norms. It's easy for people to accept the simple cause and effect of some catalysts. For instance, if a person touches a hot stove, she will quickly remove her hand or if someone sees a one-hundred-dollar bill on the street, he will probably pick it up. But when the logical result doesn't occur, people find it very difficult to accept and typically cannot believe it will happen again. Everyone has experienced the frustration of a traffic jam followed by surprise and disappointment when nothing was in the way of the cars. And that experience will occur again and again. People will slow down, perhaps to look at something on the side of the road, and drivers behind them will be surprised over and over to find they were slowed down by nothing at all.

In many ways, the stock market is an ongoing experiment tracking when people decide to press the button to buy or sell. Investors selling right away as a reaction to a crisis might be illogical or irrational, but at least people can accept it the same way we know drivers sabotage their own timeline by watching someone change a tire on the side of the road. It's far more difficult, however, to accept the speed at which investors change their minds. An everyday person walks into a room never dreaming they would electrocute someone, and it's just a matter of minutes before they are engaged in that very action. A driver slows down to look at an accident and then immediately speeds back up. An investor sells his positions and then, in just a matter of days or weeks, changes his mind and wants to buy them back.

The question isn't whether this behavior makes sense, it's if this certain catalyst consistently creates the same behavioral response. Whether it's an authority figure in a lab coat, an accident on the side of the road, or a major crisis, it seems we can predict how most people will react. Use this knowledge to put an authority figure in your life and align with a coach who will help train you to do better than your basic reactions.

▌ ACTION STEP #19: Be ready for illiquidity.

Another basic reaction to expect in difficult times is the "run on the bank" mentality that occurs in crisis. Whether it's long lines of customers trying to make withdrawals from their bank accounts or clearing all the stores of toilet paper and hand sanitizer, this behavior is a common and natural reaction to crisis. It's one of the reasons that every "prepper website" has a section dedicated to supplies that should be obtained now and stored for use later when you won't be able to get them.

Financially speaking, the item to procure now is cash, or liquidity, which brings us to an important difference between a bank account and an investment account. When you hold one hundred shares of stock in an investment account, the investment company is providing you storage services. They do not use your stock for other business purposes under penalty of fraud. If you want your stock, it's there, and it doesn't matter how many people want their stock at the same time. This means it's very easy for people to sell their shares when they feel nervous.

Banks, on the other hand, are not storage facilities. They take in deposits and lend them out, keeping only a small level of reserves required for when their customers want to make a withdrawal. Banks rely on consumer confidence to keep the system operational, and the Federal Deposit Insurance Corporation provides insurance designed to create the confidence needed for the system to keep working. If banks held all funds in storage and made them available at any time to any customer upon demand, then there would be no concerns about a "run on the bank." But in the real world, if there's a sudden lapse in banking confidence and most people want their money, the system breaks down.

The Y2K crisis, in which people worried computer software would malfunction as dates changed from the 1900s to the 2000s, turned out to be a nonevent. However, if you google the performance of the S&P 500 from December 1999 to January 2000, you'll see a clear Act of War Market Pattern in the first week of January 2000. Y2K was a systemic crisis that affected financial institutions, and investors reacted accordingly. They also withdrew so much money from banks, they would have broken the American banking system had it not been for a lucky issue of timing.

Most threatening crises are surprises and when they occur, there's a scramble to react. Y2K, on the other hand, offered the world a very important ingredient for readiness: time to prepare. With nationwide discussion about the perils of Y2K for over a year beforehand, the Federal Reserve had time to increase its cash holdings in preparation for a run on the banks. This meant that when customers made withdrawals, the Fed was able to provide the funds. The monetary supply increased dramatically at the start of 2000 because of this. Shortly after the public realized Y2K wasn't going to be the end of the world, consumers redeposited their cash, which the Fed absorbed from the banking system.

A Prepared Investor cannot rely on the Fed to be ready for the next run on the banks. Nor are the exchanges guaranteed to be always open. After 9/11, the exchanges did not open that Tuesday, and they remained closed until the following Monday in what was the longest New York Stock Exchange shutdown since 1933, when Franklin D. Roosevelt ordered it closed as part of his response to the Great Depression. It's important to have a small bit of liquidity to ease the transition as stock exchanges close and banks can't satisfy withdrawal requests.

Some people take this concept a little too far. Maybe at midnight, they're digging in their backyards, hiding gold and jewels (hopefully not diamonds). While I respect their desire to be ready for complete apocalypse, a more mainstream approach would be to use a fireproof safe in your home. By keeping enough cash to cover at least one month of your typical spending, you've created enough liquidity to weather every crisis situation that has occurred so far in modern history. Credit cards also offer a useful way to transact in times of crisis, but keep in mind those bills will have to be paid later.

ACTION STEP #20: Create your own cause-and-effect list of current events.

As discussed in the previous chapter, the way a situation is framed can be very powerful because people have a tendency to understand facts based on how they've been communicated or organized. Use this to your advantage by creating your own cause-and-effect list of the current events that you are following. Earlier in the book, we discussed the importance of keeping up with the news so that you will have a little extra time to make good choices for your finances. Let's take this a step further by framing each fact—each current event—as a question about cause and effect.

The first step to accomplish this is to expose yourself to both sides of the news cycle by coupling your sources of information. If you typically get the news from a conservative source, couple it with a more liberal one. A great technique is to try to stay informed by an even number of diverse news outlets.

The profession of journalism is an important one and considered by many to be a mandatory component of a free society. Will you get access to the brightest minds and greatest reporters for free?

Perhaps, but if we hope to continue to see their best work, society needs to support them properly. Be a paid subscriber or hire a professional who has those formal, paying connections already in place.

As discussed earlier in the book, your system should allow you to read, watch, and/or listen to the news and create a simple list of the occurrences around you. Many knowledgeable financial leaders, like Jason Zweig of the *Wall Street Journal,* have long advocated for the use of an investment diary. Here's an example of what that diary or journal might look like using a few entries from my own. Take note that without tracking the framing of the event or noticing the pattern of cause and effect, the list just feels like a bunch of ominous facts that wouldn't inform your next portfolio move.

THREE YEARS OF CURRENT EVENTS
IN CHRONOLOGICAL ORDER

January 16, 2017: Satellite images analyzed by the Washington-based Center for Strategic and International Studies show the Chinese-created islands have helipad infrastructure and the capacity to accommodate bombers.

January 27, 2017: President Trump signs executive order barring travel from seven Muslim-majority nations.

April 7, 2017: U.S. investigators reveal they are investigating Russia's involvement with Assad's most recent chemical attack in Syria.

July 8, 2017: *The Washington Post* reports that U.S. officials accuse Russian government hackers of penetrating American energy and nuclear internet networks.

July 30, 2017: Chinese leader Xi Jinping holds a major military parade just hours after U.S. President Donald Trump renewed his criticism over Beijing's failure to rein in North Korea. Perhaps coincidentally, the last weapons rolled out in the parade were China's own nuclear warhead-capable ICBMs, which state TV announcers proudly called "symbols of a major power."

August 11, 2017: Beijing warns U.S. over its Navy patrol in the South China Sea. "The American military provocation will only induce the Chinese military to further build up various defensive capacities," said Senior Col. Wu Qian, a spokesman for the Chinese Ministry of Defense.

September 22, 2017: U.S. President Donald Trump signs a new order to boost sanctions against North Korea targeting its nuclear weapons program just a few days before he threatens North Korea because the country's foreign minister, Ri Yong-ho described Mr. Trump in a fiery speech at the United Nations as a "mentally deranged person full of megalomania" on a "suicide mission."

October 23, 2017: Japan's Defense Minister asserts North Korea's nuclear missile capabilities have grown to an "unprecedented, critical and imminent" level. The minister, Itsunori Onodera, announces that this rising threat compels his country to endorse the U.S. view that "all options" must be considered. President Donald Trump states those options include military action.

November 28, 2017: North Korea tests its nuclear missile capabilities for the third time this year. The Hwasong-15 proves capable of delivering a warhead to nearly anywhere within the United States.

January 10, 2018: *The Moscow Times* reports two out of three Russians say the United States is Russia's biggest, most important enemy.

July 23, 2018: President Trump tweets to the world, "To Iranian President Rouhani: NEVER, EVER THREATEN THE UNITED STATES AGAIN OR YOU WILL SUFFER CONSEQUENCES THE LIKES OF WHICH FEW THROUGHOUT HISTORY HAVE EVER SUFFERED BEFORE."

July 30, 2018: *The Washington Post* quotes unnamed intelligence sources saying North Korea is actively constructing new intercontinental ballistic missiles at the newly renovated missile research and development facility located at Sanum-dong just a month after *The Wall Street Journal* reported North Korea broke their Summit agreement by rapidly upgrading a facility in Hamhung that produces a key component of solid-fuel missiles.

November 5, 2018: A Russian jet fighter harasses an American surveillance plane for about 25 minutes in a near-hostile encounter that U.S. officials labeled dangerous, irresponsible, and putting the pilots and crew of the U.S. plane at risk. It's thought the incident was a Russian response to the 50,000 troops, including 15,000 Americans, participating in Trident Juncture, a NATO defensive exercise in Norway designed to send a message to Moscow with a show of force at Russia's border.

November 6, 2018: Iranian President Hassan Rouhani goes on national television declaring he will put "pressure on the U.S. so it doesn't dare to continue with its plots."

April 2019: The U.S. designates the Iranian military, the elite Islamic Revolutionary Guard Corps (IRGC), a foreign "terrorist" organization, which is the first time in history Washington has formally labeled another country's military in this way. Iran quickly returns the favor, listing America a "state sponsor of terrorism" and Washington's forces as "terrorist groups."

May 2019: In the Persian Gulf, four commercial ships near the Strait of Hormuz are attacked. The United States accuses Iran of being "directly responsible" for the attacks in an area where about a fifth of the world's oil passes. Iran denies the charge.

June 6, 2019: Houthi rebels shoot down a U.S. drone in Yemen with help from Iran. Two weeks later, Iran shoots down an American drone for violating Iranian airspace. The United States denies the transgression.

August 2019: The United States formally withdraws from the Intermediate-Range Nuclear Forces Treaty with Russia stating Russia had already violated the treaty that required the two nations to limit production of short- and intermediate-range missiles.

September 14, 2019: Militant drones attack two major Saudi oil refineries, temporarily halting half the country's oil production. Though Houthi rebels claim responsibility, the United States and European powers conclude Iran is to blame. This occurs just two months after the U.S. Navy destroyed an Iranian drone in the Strait of Hormuz because it had encroached to closely to one of the American ships.

October 2019: The United States begins sending 3,000 additional troops and multiple missile defense systems to the Middle East to protect Saudi Arabia from Iranian aggression.

October 5, 2019: After eight hours of talk, the North Korea–U.S. nuclear negotiation stalls out without an agreement.

October 9, 2019: Turkey invades Syria just two days after the United States withdraws its troops from the area. Beyond the immediate military ramifications, diplomats the world over must now seriously ask if America is a reliable partner.

December 2019: Pyongyang warns America about the "Christmas gift it will . . . get." The last "gift" Pyongyang gave Washington was a nuclear test.

December 18, 2019: In response to President Trump's July 25th phone call with Ukrainian President Volodymyr Zelensky, the House of Representatives, led by Nancy Pelosi, approves two articles of impeachment despite the Senate appearing likely to quickly dismiss them.

January 3, 2020: Less than three months after U.S. Special Forces killed Abu Bakr al-Baghdadi, the leader of the Islamic State, the U.S. Department of Defense issues the following statement: "At the direction of the President, the U.S. military has taken decisive defensive action to protect U.S. personnel by killing Qasem Soleimani. General Soleimani was actively developing plans to attack American diplomats and service members in Iraq and throughout the region. General Soleimani and his Quds Force were responsible for the deaths of hundreds of American and coalition service members and the wounding of thousands more."

January 4, 2020: Gholamali Abuhamzeh, a Revolutionary Guards general, says Iran will punish Americans wherever they are within reach of the Islamic Republic.

January 7, 2020: General Soleimani achieves near-martyr status as more than fifty people are reportedly killed in a human stampede at his funeral. In all, over 200 people were injured, which is a small amount compared to the one million people who came to pay their respects in Iran's largest funeral procession since the death of Ayatollah Ruhollah Khomeini, the leader of the 1979 Islamic Revolution.

Now let's look at the same list organized by cause-and-effect where each news story is not added to the list chronologically. Instead, the news is added to the appropriate cause-and-effect situation. Each time the news offers something new, it either is added to an already existing situation or we create a new one. Looking at this revised list, it's a lot harder to feel surprised if the next crisis originates from these events. What's more, grouped together like this, it's a lot easier to sense the rising tension—the crescendo—that's slowly building toward what the public will say is an unforeseen climax in the future.

THREE YEARS OF CURRENT EVENTS
GROUPED BY CAUSE AND EFFECT

Timeline for Chinese Expansion to Control South China Sea

January 16, 2017: Satellite images analyzed by the Washington-based Center for Strategic and International Studies show the Chinese-created islands have helipad infrastructure and the capacity to accommodate bombers.

July 30, 2017: Chinese leader Xi Jinping holds a major military parade just hours after U.S. President Donald Trump renewed his criticism over Beijing's failure to rein in North Korea. Perhaps coincidentally, the last weapons rolled out in the parade were China's own nuclear warhead-capable ICBMs, which state TV announcers proudly called "symbols of a major power."

August 11, 2017: Beijing warns U.S. over its Navy patrol in the South China Sea. "The American military provocation will only induce the Chinese military to further build up various defensive capacities," said Senior Col. Wu Qian, a spokesman for the Chinese Ministry of Defense.

Timeline for American Aggression in/toward Middle East

January 27, 2017: President Trump signs executive order barring travel from seven Muslim-majority nations.

July 23, 2018: President Trump tweets to the world, "To Iranian President Rouhani: NEVER, EVER THREATEN THE UNITED STATES AGAIN OR YOU WILL SUFFER CONSEQUENCES THE LIKES OF WHICH FEW THROUGHOUT HISTORY HAVE EVER SUFFERED BEFORE."

November 6, 2018: Iranian President Hassan Rouhani goes on national television declaring he will put "pressure on the U.S. so it doesn't dare to continue with its plots."

April 2019: The U.S. designates the Iranian military, the elite Islamic Revolutionary Guard Corps (IRGC), a foreign "terrorist" organization which is the first time in history Washington has formally labeled another country's military in this way. Iran quickly returns the favor, listing America a "state sponsor of terrorism" and Washington's forces as "terrorist groups."

May 2019: In the Persian Gulf, four commercial ships near the Strait of Hormuz are attacked. The United States accuses Iran of being "directly responsible" for the attacks in an area where about a fifth of the world's oil passes. Iran denies the charge.

June 6, 2019: Houthi rebels shoot down a U.S. drone in Yemen with help from Iran. Two weeks later, Iran shoots down an American drone for violating Iranian airspace. The United States denies the transgression.

September 14, 2019: Militant drones attack two major Saudi oil refineries, temporarily halting half the country's oil production. Though Houthi rebels claim responsibility, the United States and European powers conclude Iran is to blame. This occurs just two months after the U.S. Navy destroyed an Iranian drone in the Strait of Hormuz because it had encroached to closely to one of the American ships.

October 2019: The United States begins sending 3,000 additional troops and multiple missile defense systems to the Middle East to protect Saudi Arabia from Iranian aggression.

January 3, 2020: Less than three months after U.S. Special Forces killed Abu Bakr al-Baghdadi, the leader of the Islamic State, the U.S. Department of Defense issues the following statement: "At the direction of the President, the

U.S. military has taken decisive defensive action to protect U.S. personnel by killing Qasem Soleimani. General Soleimani was actively developing plans to attack American diplomats and service members in Iraq and throughout the region. General Soleimani and his Quds Force were responsible for the deaths of hundreds of American and coalition service members and the wounding of thousands more."

January 4, 2020: Gholamali Abuhamzeh, a Revolutionary Guards general, says Iran will punish Americans wherever they are within reach of the Islamic Republic.

January 7, 2020: General Soleimani achieves near-martyr status as more than fifty people are reportedly killed in a human stampede at his funeral. In all, over 200 people were injured, which is a small amount compared to the one million people who came to pay their respects in Iran's largest funeral procession since the death of Ayatollah Ruhollah Khomeini, the leader of the 1979 Islamic Revolution.

Timeline for Russian Power-Grab Near Its Borders

April 7, 2017: U.S. investigators reveal they are investigating Russia's involvement with Assad's most recent chemical attack in Syria.

January 10, 2018: *The Moscow Times* reports two out of three Russians say the United States is Russia's biggest, most important enemy.

November 5, 2018: A Russian jet fighter harasses an American surveillance plane for about 25 minutes in a near-hostile encounter that U.S. officials labeled dangerous, irresponsible, and putting the pilots and crew of the U.S. plane at risk. It's thought the incident was a Russian response to the 50,000 troops, including 15,000 Americans, participating in Trident Juncture, a NATO defensive exercise in Norway designed to send a message to Moscow with a show of force at Russia's border.

August 2019: The United States formally withdraws from the Intermediate-Range Nuclear Forces Treaty with Russia stating Russia had already violated the treaty that required the two nations to limit production of short- and intermediate-range missiles.

October 9, 2019: Turkey invades Syria just two days after the United States withdraws its troops from the area. Beyond the immediate military ramifications, diplomats the world over must now seriously ask if America is a reliable partner.

December 18, 2019: In response to President Trump's July 25th phone call with Ukrainian President Volodymyr Zelensky, the House of Representatives, led by Nancy Pelosi, approves two articles of impeachment despite the Senate appearing likely to quickly dismiss them.

Timeline for Russian Cyber-Security Aggression

July 8, 2017: *The Washington Post* reports that U.S. officials accuse Russian government hackers of penetrating American energy and nuclear internet networks.

January 10, 2018: *The Moscow Times* reports two out of three Russians say the United States is Russia's biggest, most important enemy.

Timeline for Volatility of American Leadership

September 22, 2017: U.S. President Donald Trump signs a new order to boost sanctions against North Korea targeting its nuclear weapons program just a few days before he threatens North Korea because the country's foreign minister, Ri Yong-ho described Mr. Trump in a fiery speech at the United Nations as a "mentally deranged person full of megalomania" on a "suicide mission."

July 23, 2018: President Trump tweets to the world, "To Iranian President Rouhani: NEVER, EVER THREATEN THE UNITED STATES AGAIN OR YOU WILL SUFFER CONSEQUENCES THE LIKES OF WHICH FEW THROUGHOUT HISTORY HAVE EVER SUFFERED BEFORE."

October 5, 2019: After eight hours of talk, the North Korea–U.S. nuclear negotiation stalls out without an agreement.

October 9, 2019: Turkey invades Syria just two days after the United States withdraws its troops from the area. Beyond the immediate military ramifications, diplomats the world over must now seriously ask if America is a reliable partner.

December 18, 2019: In response to President Trump's July 25th phone call with Ukrainian President Volodymyr Zelensky, the House of Representatives, led by Nancy Pelosi, approves two articles of impeachment despite the Senate appearing likely to quickly dismiss them.

Timeline for North Korean Aggression

September 22, 2017: U.S. President Donald Trump signs a new order to boost sanctions against North Korea targeting its nuclear weapons program just a few days before he threatens North Korea because the country's foreign minister, Ri Yong-ho described Mr. Trump in a fiery speech at the United Nations as a "mentally deranged person full of megalomania" on a "suicide mission."

October 23, 2017: Japan's Defense Minister asserts North Korea's nuclear missile capabilities have grown to an "unprecedented, critical and imminent" level. The minister, Itsunori Onodera, announces that this rising threat compels his country to endorse the U.S. view that "all options" must be considered. President Donald Trump states those options include military action.

November 28, 2017: North Korea tests its nuclear missile capabilities for the third time this year. The Hwasong-15 proves capable of delivering a warhead to nearly anywhere within the United States.

July 30, 2018: *The Washington Post* quotes unnamed intelligence sources saying North Korea is actively constructing new intercontinental ballistic missiles at the newly renovated missile research and development facility located at Sanum-dong just a month after *The Wall Street Journal* reported North Korea broke their Summit agreement by rapidly upgrading a facility in Hamhung that produces a key component of solid-fuel missiles.

October 5, 2019: After eight hours of talk, the North Korea–U.S. nuclear negotiation stalls out without an agreement.

December 2019: Pyongyang warns America about the "Christmas gift it will . . . get." The last "gift" Pyongyang gave Washington was a nuclear test.

You'll notice that some of the headlines fit into multiple groups. By organizing current events by cause and effect, you've got a powerful framework for identifying a future crisis before it happens. Each time you hear something in the news, it's no longer a story in the current news cycle, it's another step forward on your cause-and-effect list. If you add in market data and notes related to the tenets of this book, you'll have a chart that looks like the following timeline for the novel corona virus crisis in 2020. Note, each entry is led with the date of the entry, the news headline, and then the S&P 500 and DJIA closing values for that day.

CASE STUDY **The COVID-19 Crisis**

"In the midst of chaos, there is also opportunity."

—SUN TZU

TIMELINE FOR THE NOVEL CORONA VIRUS

Tuesday, January 7, 2020: Officials announce they have identified a new virus, according to the WHO. The novel virus, named 2019-nCoV, was identified as belonging to the coronavirus family, which includes SARS and the common cold. S&P 500 3,237.18—DJIA 28,583.68

Prepared Investor Notes: I am following the World Health Organization as an organization/leader of influence, so this is how the news enters my spreadsheet. I note it as a new virus, but this is a systemic crisis and therefore will not affect the stock market unless it clearly/directly impacts the economy by doing something like destroying financial infrastructure. Further, while the virus itself is new, society won't be shocked by it because a respiratory virus originating from China is not new at all. No action taken.

Friday, January 17, 2020: A second death is reported in Wuhan, health authorities in the U.S. announce that three airports will start screening passengers arriving from the city. S&P 500 3,329.62—DJIA 29,348.10

Prepared Investor Notes: This is no longer just a "China-only thing." USA is screening for it at airports. But this has happened before so investors will not panic over this. Need to see economic impact that the regular public can understand/get scared of. Still no action.

Thursday, January 23, 2020: Wuhan, Hubei, and another province placed under quarantine. S&P 500 3,325.54—DJIA 29,160.09

Prepared Investor Notes: Quarantine is both new and affects financial infrastructure because of supply chain disruption. The most conservative Prepared Investors might take action today/tomorrow to protect themselves or by readying for a drop and subsequent rise. Less conservative views would still wait to see if this quarantine phenomenon goes beyond China. Since that is not likely, no action taken.

Friday, January 24, 2020: The number of cities under lockdown in Hubei rose to 13, affecting 41 million people. S&P 500 3,295.47—DJIA 28,989.73

Prepared Investor Notes: Quarantine is the crisis. It is new and affects millions. The Prepared Investor notices and expects that a really conservative Prepared Investor might take steps according to their risk levels. But for me, the question remains if this is being framed as only a Chinese problem/phenomenon. If that framework changes, there could be panic. No action taken.

Thursday, January 30, 2020: WHO Director-General Tedros Adhanom Ghebreyesus declares the 2019-nCoV outbreak a public health emergency of international concern, noting the potential spread of the virus to countries with weak healthcare systems. The decision comes as more countries outside China report cases of infection, including the Philippines and India. Both confirm their first 2019-nCoV cases. Total confirmed cases in China reach 9,692, with 213 deaths. WHO recommends "2019-nCoV acute respiratory disease" as interim name for the disease. S&P 500 3,283.66—DJIA 28,859.44

Prepared Investor Notes: I'm following WHO as an organization/leader of influence, so this information is noted. But, because a systemic threat, such as a virus, doesn't alarm investors by itself, still looking for direct impact to economy or financial infrastructure. Still looking at how this is framed. It appears the USA thinks the quarantine is only a Chinese problem.

Wednesday, February 5, 2020: Ten passengers from a cruise ship currently docked in Yokohama, Japan, test positive for 2019-nCoV, bringing the total cases in Japan to 35, now the highest among countries with confirmed cases outside mainland China. Global cases total over 28,000, with 565 deaths, and a majority of cases in China. S&P 500 3,334.69—DJIA 29,290.85

Prepared Investor Notes: Identifying the travel industry as possible buying opportunity. Thinking of cruises, airlines, and hotels.

Saturday, February 8, 2020: WHO Director General T. A. Ghebreyesus criticizes the levels of misinformation spreading around the virus, saying "we're not just battling the virus; we're also battling the trolls and conspiracy theorists that push misinformation and undermine the outbreak response." He says WHO is engaging with Facebook, Google, Tencent, Baidu, Twitter, TikTok, Weibo, Pinterest, and others to promote accurate information about 2019-nCoV. S&P 500 3,327.71—DJIA 29,102.51

Prepared Investor Notes: The last virus hit over 10 years ago and these social media engines didn't have the same global power they do today. This sounds like a change to the framing. People are going to be immediately aware of the up-to-the-minute virus news, which could lead to a more aggressive fear response if the virus crosses out of a systemic crisis that is not affecting the markets. So far, the indices show they are unaffected.

Sunday, February 9, 2020: Death toll in China surpasses that of the 2002–2003 SARS epidemic, with 811 deaths recorded. S&P 500 3,327.71—DJIA 29,102.51

Prepared Investor Notes: The deadliness of the crisis is not the market driver. Small or large, it's people's perception of the situation. People need to believe they can get it, something like the lottery effect. Doesn't look like anything will come of it. No action taken.

Tuesday, February 11, 2020: WHO Director General T. A. Ghebreyesus calls the outbreak a "very grave threat for the rest of the world." S&P 500 3,357.75—DJIA 29,276.34

Prepared Investor Notes: I agree it's "a very grave threat" but not for my portfolio unless this hits financial infrastructure or the economy or there's some other major change/development in situational framing.

Friday, February 14, 2020: WHO says that, overall, the percentage of health workers infected with COVID-19 is lower than what has occurred historically in outbreaks of other kinds of coronaviruses. S&P 500 3,380.16—DJIA 29,398.08

Prepared Investor Notes: WHO says it's not so bad, but this doesn't matter. Some will agree and some won't. How framed? Not a major American problem. No action taken.

Saturday, February 15, 2020: News reports that google searches on coronavirus have significantly dropped since January. S&P 500 3,380.16—DJIA 29,398.08

Prepared Investor Notes: It appears people are losing interest in the virus. This could be the last entry for this timeline.

Tuesday, February 18, 2020: Russia now bans entry for Chinese citizens starting February 20. S&P 500 3,370.29—DJIA 29,232.19

Prepared Investor Notes: Framing sounds like a Russian/Chinese issue. No action needed.

Sunday, February 23, 2020: Neighboring countries close their borders with Iran due to fears of the outbreak spreading. S&P 500 3,337.75—DJIA 28,992.41

Prepared Investor Notes: Borders closing, plus multiple CEOs have announced recently that their companies are affected by COVID-19. Supply chain interruption—is this too complex to impact the public overall? Also, what if someone important in financial world dies of COVID? Who could this be? The U.S. president . . . who else? No action now.

Tuesday, February 25, 2020: The U.S. Centers for Disease Control and Prevention warns about the likely spread of COVID-19 in the United States, urging the population to "prepare for the expectation that this might be bad." Dr. Nancy Messonnier, director at the National Center for Immunization and Respiratory Diseases, cautioned during a press briefing: "It's not so much of a question of if this will happen anymore but rather more of a question of exactly when this will happen." S&P 500 3,128.21—DJIA 27,081.36

Prepared Investor Notes: Could be a seed for a change to the framing of this situation. CDC says virus is coming, but that's not new and markets won't react without additional cause.

Thursday, February 27, 2020: USA is considering invoking the Defense Production Act, which grants President Trump the power to expand industrial production of key materials or products for national security. S&P 500 2,978.76—DJIA 25,766.64

Prepared Investor Notes: Can Donald Trump, with his volatile outbursts, affect this market? If he invokes this DPA, will it frighten investors? Probably not, but remaining vigilant.

Friday, February 28, 2020: WHO officials say it is not yet time to declare a pandemic, adding that once one is declared, efforts will move away from containment to mitigation. S&P 500 2,954.22—DJIA 25,409.36

Prepared Investor Notes: This is framing and the word doesn't matter. Academics don't call it a pandemic but regular people see this as global now. If it seriously affects financial infrastructure, a major leader dies of it, or if it directly impacts the economy, then this is how it will bring people together strongly enough to create panic and cause the markets to fall. Market is slightly down but could be unrelated. No action taken.

Saturday, February 29, 2020: News reports major travel bans and denial of entry could have a significant economic and social impact. S&P 500 2,954.22—DJIA 25,409.36

Prepared Investor Notes: Possible further problems for travel industry. Staying focused on opportunities there.

Saturday, February 29, 2020: U.S. reports first death on American soil. S&P 500 2,954.22—DJIA 25,409.36

Prepared Investor Notes: Not going to drop the market, but very interesting how quickly everyone seems to know about it. Social media definitely is ramping up the emotional component that is a part of every crisis—it's not a crisis yet, maybe it won't be, but if it becomes one, social media could create a lottery effect where it feels like it's touching everyone.

Monday, March 2, 2020: Influenza is different from COVID-19 because there are treatments, vaccines, and there is an understanding of its transmission and patterns, says Dr. Michael Ryan, executive director at the WHO Health Emergencies Programme, during a press conference. "Here we have a disease in which we have no vaccine, no treatment, we don't fully understand transmission, we don't really understand case fatality. What we have been genuinely heartened by is that unlike influenza, where countries have fought back, where they've put in place strong measures, we've remarkably seen that the virus is suppressed." S&P 500 3,090.23—DJIA 26,703.32

Prepared Investor Notes: So, this is just like SARS, MERS, H1N1 . . . it's not going to unite investors in panicked selling without additional help.

Wednesday, March 4, 2020: The United Nations Educational, Scientific and Cultural Organization says COVID-19 has disrupted the education of 290.5 million students globally, which is an "unprecedented" figure. This includes school closures in 13 countries. S&P 500 3,130.12—DJIA 27,090.86

Prepared Investor Notes: School closures due to a virus is new. If this hits the U.S. in a meaningful way, it could be a spark worth considering depending on how it's framed. But, at its core, society does not view this as directly impacting the economy. No action taken.

Friday, March 6, 2020: WHO says there are more than 200 clinical trials registered that look at different therapeutics to treat COVID-19, as well as traditional Chinese medicine, according to Dr. Maria Van Kerkhove, technical lead of the WHO Health Emergencies Programme. S&P 500 2,972.37—DJIA 25,864.78

Prepared Investor Notes: A treatment is coming, just like with other viruses in the past. Probably last entry for this timeline.

Sunday, March 8, 2020: Italy places 60 million residents on lockdown. S&P 500 2,972.37—DJIA 25,864.78

Prepared Investor Notes: CRISIS catalyst here. Quarantine is new to the west, and it's the virus making the leap to directly affecting the stock market. Businesses closed, supply chains disrupted, and there's no end date in sight. People will understand this. The spark is here. Let's hope it's not a bad drop/

panic. Note that 2,972 is our S&P closing value to use for any plans to protect or grow portfolios.

Reading through this timeline, it's hard to feel surprised by the crisis. It's more just a process of waiting to see if. . . . This proactive approach is the same thing as keeping your eyes on the road and your hands on the wheel while driving a car. If you see debris in the street, you try to avoid it. If you hit it, you listen for the flapping of a tire losing air. When the signs are there, you have to pull over and start doing the work you practiced because you wanted to be ready for this exact situation. The following timeline is an example of that work. It starts with the declaration of crisis and provides both an in-depth look at how we "change the tire" and a conclusion to the novel corona virus case study.

FURTHER TIMELINE FOR THE NOVEL CORONA VIRUS

Sunday, March 8, 2020: Italy places 60 million residents on lockdown. S&P 500 2,972.37—DJIA 25,864.78

Prepared Investor Notes: CRISIS catalyst here. Note that 2,972 is our S&P closing value to use for any plans to protect or grow portfolios.

Monday, March 9, 2020: Russia and Saudi Arabia begin a concerted effort to push an agenda focused on "no control on oil flow." S&P 500 2,746.56—DJIA 23,851.02

Prepared Investor Notes: CRISIS catalyst here. This entry is from an altogether different cause-and-effect timeline. This is a leader-driven crisis as these countries purposefully aim to drive down the price of oil, hurting the U.S. oil industry. This means two separate crisis sparks in just a couple days. Nevertheless, 2,972 is still our starting figure for reaction plans. Due to two separate catalysts, recommending that, for those who typically take action at 7 to 9 percent down, consider actions at 14 to 18 percent down. This would be in the high 2,400's for the S&P 500. This might not be the bottom of a future decline, but it's a great place to take advantage of panicked sales if there are any.

Wednesday, March 11, 2020: The U.K. announces up to $192.4 million (£150 million) in aid funding from the nation's budget to "mitigate the impact of coronavirus on the world's most vulnerable countries." S&P 500 2,741.38—DJIA 23,553.22

> *Prepared Investor Notes:* Wow, this is a fast response. All of my social media is focused on COVID only—it's all that is trending on Twitter. Orders were made on Monday to make purchases just below 2,500 on the S&P 500. Still waiting.

Thursday, March 12, 2020: The Pacific Islands confirms its first case is a patient who came from Paris. S&P 500 2,480.64—DJIA 21,200.62

> *Prepared Investor Notes:* High 2400's happens today. Purchases made *en masse*. Looking for a 7 percent rise to take advantage of and pad the portfolio. So exit point is around 2,650. Some people may want less or more rise.

Friday, March 13, 2020: A U.S. national emergency is declared over the novel corona virus outbreak. S&P 500 2,711.02—DJIA 23,185.62

> *Prepared Investor Notes:* Trump makes National Emergency announcement, and since he's been trying to frame this virus situation as nothing to be alarmed about, this announcement is met with happiness that he's doing something. The market has risen. I'm unsure he's influential enough to stem the tide though. Will it continue to drop? Likely. With current rise, closing out short-term tactical positions where it makes sense. This creates a nice profit that adds to the portfolio and helps to keep the overall portfolio from performing poorly if the market does badly in the months ahead.

Thursday, March 19, 2020: Nearly all U.S. states declare a state of emergency. S&P 500 2,409.39—DJIA 20,087.19

> *Prepared Investor Notes:* Now, we are in "further bad news." We don't want to mistake this aftermath as a crisis catalyst. We know the story, and it's going to be hard living through it as it unfolds. There's already "quarantine life" phraseology. We don't like it, but we're adapting. This crisis is real, but like all crises it cannot last forever.

A Prepared Investor has a month of cash at the ready and a third party who they trust to help them during tough times. Prepared Investors pay attention to current events and arrange the information in a way that allows them to better understand the world unfolding around them. With these techniques, we use our natural inclinations to our own advantage. In the next chapter, we review all the activities necessary to become a Prepared Investor and conclude with the most important action step of all.

CHAPTER EIGHT

"We Will Face a Terrible Day"
The Most Important Action Step of All

Pulitzer Prize winner Peggy Noonan wrote in the *Wall Street Journal*, "You can't see all the world's weapons and all its madness and not know that eventually we will face a terrible day or days . . . Maybe it will involve nuclear weapons . . . an attack on the grid, maybe bioterrorism. But it will be bad . . ." If one believes a future crisis is currently brewing in the present, then it makes sense to prepare. Finding and defining the Act of War Market Pattern has been an exhausting effort involving many people, but it shouldn't be so difficult to take action now that the pattern is so clear. In fact, just as people have a diversity of viewpoints about how to react to standard financial news, so too are there many possible ways to take advantage of the Act of War Market Pattern after identifying the onset of a major crisis. The argument over which approach is the most advantageous has just begun, and to help further the discussion, here are some simple questions to consider.

When doing portfolio transactions in the face of crisis, why limit the orders to a market movement of 7 percent as seen in the provided case studies? Why not 8 or 9 percent? Why limit the margin to only thirty percent of the portfolio? If thirty is good, why not 45 or 60 percent? Why use leveraged ETFs? Why not use options to control more of the market with fewer dollars? These changes could make the profit larger, and for some, that's a compelling reason to take action. Going the other way with less risk and less profit might be compelling as well to certain readers. Although there are a variety of methods to take advantage of the Act of War Market Pattern, there remains the difficulty of maintaining the discipline to wait for these infrequent occurrences. The rarity of the Act of War Market Pattern makes this book all the more important because it helps readers delineate their own strategy today so they will be ready when the next major crisis occurs tomorrow.

No one knows if the next collective threat will come from North Korean nuclear warheads, from an enhanced Chinese Navy, or from Russian cyberattacks. But when the next major crisis occurs, it's certain investors will be affected and the conversation for how to protect wealth needs to be different. In the past, Wall Street has suggested "buy and hold" because someday the crisis will be over and the investment markets will return to normal. But that dogma doesn't function as well now that there's clearly a better approach. The simple fact is people cannot "unfind" a pattern once they understand it. Patterns are the most basic memory aid and why it's easy to memorize a song or to know what comes next in the phrase, "Two, Four, Six . . ."

If it wasn't a uniformed scientific authority asking the volunteers to shock someone in a different room, they wouldn't have pressed the button. If JFK had not been shot, the $11 billion drop would not have happened. If it hadn't been Napoleon personally looking the French soldiers in the eye, offering his breast as a target, they wouldn't have surrendered. Identifying the exact catalyst matters. A major threat such as a man-made crisis or act of war is an intentional conflict creating a perceived danger for which evolution has prepared a particular human reaction. People just don't feel the same despair, challenge, or fear in reaction to a tornado or a backyard pool because these things aren't consciously trying to attack anyone. Fear of death, therefore, is less powerful than fear of an attack, meaning an understanding of serious crises from a financial perspective is less about the actual mortal danger and much more dependent on the number of people who feel frightened by it.

Author of *Sapiens: A Brief History of Humankind*, Yuval Noah Harari seeks to answer questions about why human beings dominate the planet so completely. Typically, after any achievement, people attribute the success to the individuals involved, citing their talents or perseverance. Harari takes an opposite approach, suggesting the reason humans are elevated above all other animals isn't found on the individual level at all. He believes it is humankind's collective abilities that are the key.

Harari offers an example of someone who is stuck on a remote island with a chimpanzee. In this situation, an individual's intelligence or physical superiority offers little advantage in a simple, one-on-one contest between a chimpanzee and a person. In fact, it's very likely that, in this situation, an enraged chimpanzee would seriously injure and perhaps kill most human beings.

Harari proposes that humans control the planet because they are the only animals capable of cooperating both flexibly and in very large numbers. He offers examples such as the bees and the ants who can cooperate in large numbers but fail to do so flexibly. Their cooperation is rigid, meaning there is only one way in which a beehive can function. If a new opportunity or danger arises, the ants cannot have a revolution one evening and the next day a capitalistic society emerges following a new ant leader. In contrast, humans can flexibly cooperate using extremely sophisticated and effective networks of communication. Whether it's building the Great Wall of China or operating equipment on Mars by remote control, Harari believes the major accomplishments of humankind have not been based on individual abilities, but on how we work together.

There is, however, one hive of human activity requiring people to behave without our normal cooperation. In a kind of voluntary de-evolution, this one special system forces humans backward to a point where individuals are forced to interact in a far less than optimum way. This one interesting collective is constantly changing the rules to punish individuals who try to game the system to get ahead. In this particular "hive," human beings must ultimately act on their own, despite all the intelligence and information sharing that encourages people to participate.

This incredible experiment is, of course, the stock market, and its unpredictability is the result of hundreds of millions of individual points of view. In the market's daily auction, people must buy and sell with their individual dollars and then, collectively, the results unfold for all to see how they have fared. Insider trading is illegal, and government watchdogs constantly monitor for any form of cooperation that could be considered market manipulation.

It's so difficult to predict the collective results from all these individual decisions that people get doctorates dedicated to this very idea. Traders, fund managers, and economists commit their lives to trying to explain the movement of the stock market and predict its next move. When they get it just a little bit right, they win Nobel Prizes and are celebrated in the media. With just one seemingly lucky trade, a hedge fund manager can open the door to millions of dollars from other investors who want the manger to get it right again, but with their money this time. The news is full of investment advisors and hedge fund managers who succeeded in one great bet they could never repeat.

The only time the stock market behaves predictably is when this machine of individuals reacts in the same way to a similar catalyst. Because of humankind's vast range of perspectives and magnificent variety of motivations, this predictable behavior is extremely rare. But, as a chapter by chapter examination of major crises demonstrates, there is one situation in which people buy or sell with a startling predictability: at the onset of a collective threat or crisis. Like a beehive reacting to a bear reaching in to steal some honey, this particular catalyst touches the American investor in such a way that, despite religion, politics, wealth, or geographic location, they engage in an obvious pattern that dissipates after individual needs and motivations take over again.

Over the years, Wall Street has embraced a few basic tenets as the investing public came to understand them. For example, investors know diversification leads to lower risk and higher return because the pattern was uncovered and published. Investors know blue chip stocks are generally less risky than small cap stocks because the pattern was proven and shared. Stocks are typically riskier than bonds. It's time to add one more rule of thumb. Stocks predictably fall and quickly bounce back following the start of a threatening crisis in a phenomenon known as the Act of War Market Pattern.

In conclusion, let's review the twenty basic steps to be ready for the next crisis from a financial perspective:

ACTION STEP #1: Identify the two types of crisis that affect the stock market: threatening and systemic.

ACTION STEP #2: Know how to identify irreversible systemic change even if, in the short term, the stock market does not.

ACTION STEP #3: Save everything first. Then, schedule your designated monthly spending.

ACTION STEP #4: Don't use your savings to buy things that cost money. Instead, buy things that make money.

ACTION STEP #5: Recognize the Act of War Market Pattern.

ACTION STEP #6: Remain calm and thoughtful to avoid emotional mistakes.

ACTION STEP #7: Seek privacy to keep your options open.

ACTION STEP #8: Keep an Ideas List to guide your future investment efforts beyond simple war machine modernization to include the recently famous and shortage-induced disrupters.

ACTION STEP #9: Regularly update your list of world leaders and follow their movements.

ACTION STEP #10: Don't let good times affect your vigilance.

ACTION STEP #11: Make your reaction plan right now.

ACTION STEP #12: Recognize irrational investor behavior when society reacts instinctually to a threat.

ACTION STEP #13: Don't mistake "more bad news" as a new, or second, crisis.

ACTION STEP #14: Recognize how the public's crisis-centric mentality affects certain companies or industries a lot more than others.

ACTION STEP #15: Know your risk tolerance.

ACTION STEP #16: Consider situational framing to help identify if society perceives a crisis.

ACTION STEP #17: Use social experience to help read the room and identify if society perceives a crisis.

ACTION STEP #18: Find a coach.

ACTION STEP #19: Be ready for illiquidity.

ACTION STEP #20: Create your own cause-and-effect list of current events.

"When we look back on all the perils through which we have passed and at the mighty foes that we have laid low and all the dark and deadly designs that we have frustrated, why should we fear for our future? We have come safely through the worst."
—Winston Churchill

The one step missing from this book might be the most important action step of all, especially for those of us who are worried about war, terrorism, and cyberattacks. *Have the courage to stay positive!* Just because something bad—some kind of terrible crisis—is looming, it does not mean we need to live our lives in fear. We can see the pattern of current events spiraling up into an inevitable conflict of some sort and must remember this: these dark worries, while legitimate, quickly dissipate with the bright knowledge that we've been through crisis before. We've withstood major calamity, and we'll do it again. Will it be easy? Will it be without tragedy? Of course not, but that doesn't mean there will be utter loss and total annihilation.

Situational framing can help you stay positive. Imagine the perspective of someone who was born in the year 1900. When she turned fourteen, World War I was just beginning and shortly after, she has to deal with the Spanish flu until she's in her twenties. Before she's thirty years old, the Great Depression begins and, just when she's got that in the rearview mirror, World War II starts. Before she's sixty-five years old, she's endured the Korean War, the Vietnam War, and the assassination of JFK. Like Fred Rogers of the TV Show *Mr. Roger's Neighborhood* says, "There is no normal life that is free of pain. . . . How great it is when we come to know that times of disappointment can be followed by joy."

Consider the aging athlete—a professional baseball catcher—who takes the field, game after game. Is there any guarantee he'll win? When he suits up for the next game, what promise does he have that he won't get hurt? The catcher keeps getting older, but whether he's in his home field or at an away game, he still kneels in the dust and keeps his eyes on the ball right up until the moment it slams into his mitt. Isn't it reasonable to expect an injury to happen at some point? Will every game be without tragedy? Perhaps these questions are what make the game worth playing in the first place.

A Prepared Investor is very similar to this major league catcher, taking throw after throw, ever at the ready for an opposing player to try to steal second base. The pitcher steps up to the mound, nods at your signal, and throws a three-inch baseball one hundred miles per hour directly into your outstretched glove. At the moment the ball seats into your catcher's mitt, most people would blink and flinch a little bit. It's a natural reaction that's very hard to avoid, and if every ticketholder at a Yankee's game left the stands to play catcher for one pitch, the odds are all of them would blink when the ball hits the glove. Pitch after pitch. Person after person.

But not everyone blinks.

With specific training, that professional catcher sits ready for the ball, eyes open, and aware of the runners already on the bases. We know the rules because we've studied history and have seen the way the game is played. We know the basic cause and effect. We accept facts like how the baseball travels sixty feet and six inches from the pitcher's mound in only 400 milliseconds, and, if we blink, we'll be blind for almost that entire time. We understand the steps we have to take and the things we need to practice. We don't have to get ready for the preposterous. We just need the courage to suit up and make sure we don't blink.

We just need to be prepared.

Acknowledgments

Being prepared is a lot easier when you are surrounded by topnotch people, and the same is true when writing a book. My team at work is my second family, and I'm filled with gratitude every time I walk through the door at Manske Wealth Management. I'm also grateful to the wonderful staff, presenters, and attendees at the various writer's conferences across the country such as The Writer's Digest Writer's Conference, the San Francisco Writer's Conference, the Pacific Northwest Writer's Conference, and the New York Writer's Workshop. Tom Tomlinson and all the attendees at the NYWW were very helpful in honing my description of this project. I met Meghan Stevenson at the San Francisco Writer's Conference and am so lucky she agreed to help edit the book—thank you, Meghan! I'm extremely thankful to Amber Gruen for her critique of the manuscript, which set such a high bar for my other beta readers (thank you to all!). In Houston, Jason Jimenez and the many professionals collaborating with me in Business Networking International helped me with referrals, which is how I met Randy Peyser, who did a great job spreading the word on *The Prepared Investor* at BookExpo in New York. I was honored to receive a number of very positive endorsements from some very amazing people all over the country, and I'm very grateful to each of them for their support. I'm compelled to thank Francesca Minerva and Pat Campisi. Francesca is a veteran in the publishing industry, a great agent, and a tough cookie who can laugh in the face of any storm. So glad she's in my corner. If it was my mind and hands writing this book, my outstanding research team was the heart and blood keeping me going. Thank you especially to Jordan

Fandry and Lisa Fierro, who put in over one hundred hours creating charts and scouring various libraries, online databases, and university resources to help make sure my facts were accurate. I am proud to be published by Changing Lives Press and thankful to all the great professionals I've met through CLP, including Michele Matrisciani and Carol K. Rosenberg. They are both word wizards and I'm so grateful for your time and attention! A few more acknowledgments: Whether stories, songs, or poems, my father has a deep respect for the written word, and I'm grateful he provided one of the first informal critiques of this book. My mother greatly enjoys reading and, growing up, our home always had books in it. I'm extremely thankful to them both for their many gifts! Finally, it took almost ten years to research, write, redraft, review, revise, and finally publish this book. During this time, my wife Jessica (YAIMH) and my daughters Charlotte, Avery, Amelia, and Adriana (three hand squeezes) were a constant source of strength, support, and love. Thank you!

References

WORLD WAR I

America's Story from America's Library. "World War I Ended With the Treaty of Versailles June 28, 1919." Accessed July 15, 2015. www.americaslibrary.gov/jb/jazz/jb_jazz_ww1_1. html.

Cooper, J.M. "Woodrow Wilson: Overview." *The New York Times.* October 1, 2010. Accessed July 15, 2015. topics.nytimes.com/top/reference/timestopics/people/w/woodrow_wilson/index.html.

Cosgrove, Ben. (2014, July 16). "A Picture Before Dying: Franz Ferdinand and Sophie, Sarajevo, 1914." *TIME.* Retrieved on July 15, 2015 from http://time.com/3880415/margaret-macmillan-on-assassination-of-franz-ferdinand-and-sophie/

FindLaw. "US v. Forty Barrels and Twenty Kegs of Coca Cola." Accessed June 29, 2015. caselaw.findlaw.com/us-supreme-court/241/265.html.

Fitzgerald, Gerard J. "Chemical Warfare and Medical Response During World War I." *American Journal of Public Health* 98, no. 4 (April 2008):611–625. doi:10.2105/AJPH.2007.11930.

FOOD BILL IS SIGNED. The Statesman (1916–1921), August 10, 1917. Retrieved from http://search.proquest.com/docview/1617427653?accountid=5682

Ghizoni, Sandra Kollen. "Reserve Banks Open for Business." Federal Reserve History. November 22, 2013. Accessed July 16, 2015. www.federalreservehistory.org/Events/DetailView/18.

History.com. "Ku Klux Klan." Accessed July 15, 2015. www.history.com/topics/ku-klux-klan.

IMDb. "The Birth of a Nation (1915)." Accessed July 15, 2015. www.imdb.com/title/tt0004972/.

King, Gilbert. "Sabotage in New York Harbor." Smithsonian. November 1, 2011. Accessed July 15, 2015. www.smithsonianmag.com/history/sabotage-in-new-york-harbor-123968672/?no-ist.

Lerner, Michael A. "Going Dry: The Coming of Prohibition." *Humanities* Magazine. September/October 2011. Accessed July 4, 2020. www.neh.gov/humanities/2011/septemberoctober/feature/going-dry.

Library of Congress. "Lafayette Escadrille: Topics in Chronicling America." Library of

Congress Research Guides. March 18, 2013. Accessed June 26, 2015. www.loc.gov/rr/news/topics/escadrille.html.

Library of Congress. "Zimmerman Telegram: Topics in Chronicling America." The Library of Congress Research Guides. September 23, 2014. Accessed July 15, 2015. www.loc.gov/rr/news/topics/zimmerman.html.

"Many Explosions Since War Began," July 31, 1916. *New York Times* (1857–1922) Accessed July 15, 2015. http://search.proquest.com/docview/97877593?accountid=5682.

National Aeronautics and Space Administration. "Aeronautics and Astronautics Chronology, 1915-1919." NASA.gov. Accessed June 26, 2015. www.hq.nasa.gov/office/pao/History/Timeline/1915-19.html.

National Archives. "Military Records: World War I Selective Service System Draft Registration Cards, M1509." Last reviewed July 15, 2019. Accessed July 15, 2015. www.archives.gov/research/military/ww1/draft-registration/.

National Constitution Center. "Prohibition of Liquor." Accessed July 16, 2015. constitutioncenter.org/constitution/the-amendments/amendment-18-liquor-abolished.

November 28—World War I: Following a war-induced closure in July, the New York Stock Exchange re-opens for bond trading. http://www.businessinsider.com/world-war-i-impact-on-markets-2014-8

OurDocuments.gov. "Servicemen's Readjustment Act (1944)." Accessed June 26, 2020. www.ourdocuments.gov/doc.php?flash=false&doc=76.

Ravitz, Jessica. "Murder Case, Leo Frank Lynching Live On." CNN. November 2, 2009. Accessed July 15, 2015. www.cnn.com/2009/CRIME/11/02/leo.frank/index.html?eref=rss_us.

Ray, Michael. "U-boat: German Submarine." Encyclopædia Britannica Online. Accessed July 16, 2015. www.britannica.com/technology/U-boat.

Sides, Hampton. "Erik Larson's 'Dead Wake,' About the Lusitania." *The New York Times*. March 5, 2015. Accessed July 15, 2015. www.nytimes.com/2015/03/08/books/review/erik-larsons-dead-wake-about-the-lusitania.html?_r=2.

Time Magazine. "Nation: The Various Shady Lives of the Ku Klux Klan." April 9, 1965. Accessed July 4, 2020. content.time.com/time/magazine/article/0,9171,898581,00.html.

The U.S. Department of State. "Purchase of the United States Virgin Islands, 1917." Accessed June 29, 2015. 2001-2009.state.gov/r/pa/ho/time/wwi/107293.htm.

The U.S. Department of State, Office of the Historian. "Milestones: 1914–1920: US Entry into World War I, 1917." Accessed July 1, 2015. history.state.gov/milestones/1914-1920/wwi.

Williamson, Samuel H. "Daily Closing Value of the Dow Jones Average in the United States, May 2, 1885 to Present." Measuring Worth. Accessed July 4, 2020. www.measuringworth.com/datasets/DJA/.

Wormser, Richard. "Jim Crow Stories: D.W. Griffith's The Birth of a Nation (1915)." PBS. Accessed July 15, 2015. www.pbs.org/wnet/jimcrow/stories_events_birth.html.

Yale Law School. "8 January, 1918: President Woodrow Wilson's Fourteen Points." The Avalon Project. Accessed July 15, 2015. avalon.law.yale.edu/20th_century/wilson14.asp.

WORLD WAR II

Andrews, Evan. "5 Attacks on US Soil During World War II." History Lists. October 23, 2012. Accessed July 8, 2015. www.history.com/news/history-lists/5-attacks-on-u-s-soil-during-world-war-ii.

Burtness, Paul S., and Warren U. Ober. "Communication Lapses Leading to the Pearl Harbor Disaster." *Historian* 75, no. 4 (November 2013):740–759. doi:10.1111/hisn.12019.

Burtness, Paul S., and Warren U. Ober. "President Roosevelt, Admiral Stark, and the Unsent Warning to Pearl Harbor: A Research Note." *Australian Journal Of Politics & History* 57, no. 4 (December 2011): 580–588. doi:10.1111/j.1467-8497.2011.01615.x.

Burtness, Paul S., and Warren U. Ober. "Three MacArthur Letters on the Philippine Disaster: A Research Note." *Australian Journal of Politics & History* 55, no. 4 (December 2009): 544–56. doi.org/10.1111/j.1467-8497.2009.01532.x.

Butow, R.J.C. "How Roosevelt Attacked Japan at Pearl Harbor: Myth Masquerading as History." *Prologue Magazine*. Fall 1996, Vol. 28, No. 3. Accessed July 24, 2015. www.archives.gov/publications/prologue/1996/fall/butow.html.

CNN Library. "World War II Fast Facts." September 1, 2014. Accessed July 1, 2015. www.cnn.com/2013/07/09/world/world-war-ii-fast-facts/.

Cullen, K. Einstein, Albert. In Science online. Retrieved from http://www.fofweb.com/activelink2.asp?ItemID=WE40&SID=5&iPin=PSP0006&SingleRecord=True

Federal Register- Franklin D. Roosevelt—1940. National Archives. Retrieved July 24, 2015 from http://www.archives.gov/federal-register/executive-orders/1940.html#8389

Goldstein, Richard. "Fred Korematsu, 86, Dies; Lost Key Suit on Internment." *The New York Times*. April 1, 2005. Accessed August 10, 2015. www.nytimes.com/2005/04/01/us/fred-korematsu-86-dies-lost-key-suit-on-internment.html?_r=0.

Gosling, F.G. "The Manhattan Project: Making the Atomic Bomb." Department of Energy. Accessed July 4, 2020. www.energy.gov/management/downloads/gosling-manhattan-project-making-atomic-bomb.

Harsch, Joseph C. "Pearl Harbor Dec. 7, 1941; A Reporter Remembers . . ." *The Christian Science Monitor*. December 7, 1981. Accessed July 22, 2015. www.csmonitor.com/1981/1207/120765.html.

History. "Japanese Task Force Leaves for Pearl Harbor." Accessed July 23, 2015. www.history.com/this-day-in-history/japanese-task-force-leaves-for-pearl-harbor#.

Holocaust Encyclopedia. "The Holocaust and World War II: Key Dates." United States Holocaust Memorial Museum. Accessed August 3, 2015. www.ushmm.org/wlc/en/article.php?ModuleId=10007653.

The Japanese American National Museum. "Chronology of WWII Incarceration." Accessed August 10, 2015. www.janm.org/projects/clasc/chronology.htm.

"Japanese bomb found in Oregon is linked to unidentified seaplane." *New York Times*, September 15, 1942 (1923–Current File) Retrieved from http://search.proquest.com/docview/106310041?accountid=5682

Klein, Christopher. "8 Things You May Not Know About Daylight Saving Time."

History. March 9, 2012. Accessed December 8, 2015. www.history.com/news/8-things -you-may-not-know-about-daylight-saving-time.

Morton, Louis. "Chapter 4: Japan's Decision for War." US Army Center of Military History. Accessed July 23, 2015. www.history.army.mil/books/70-7_04.htm.

The National WWII Museum New Orleans. "The Battle of Iwo Jima." Accessed August 12, 2015. www.nationalww2museum.org/focus-on/iwo-jima-fact-sheet.pdf.

The Nobel Prize. "Albert Einstein: Biographical." NobelPrize.org. Accessed July 10, 2015. www.nobelprize.org/nobel_prizes/physics/laureates/1921/einstein-bio.html.

NPR. "A Pearl Harbor Timeline." December 7, 2004. Accessed July 28, 2015. www.npr.org/ templates/story/story.php?storyId=4206060.

NPR. "Timeline: The Road to Hiroshima." August 5, 2005. Accessed July 8, 2015. www.npr. org/templates/story/story.php?storyId=4785786.

PBS. "Children of the Camps Internment History: WWII Internment Timeline." Accessed August 10, 2015. www.pbs.org/childofcamp/history/timeline.html.

Robbins, Ted. "A Japanese Attack Before Pearl Harbor." NPR. December 13, 2007. Accessed July 14, 2015. http://www.npr.org/templates/story/story.php?storyId=17110447.

Stromberg, Joseph. "After Pearl Harbor, Vandals Cut Down Four of DC's Japanese Cherry Trees." *Smithsonian Magazine*. April 7, 2014. Accessed June 26, 2020. www.smithsonianmag.com/ history/after-pearl-harbor-vandals-cut-down-four-dcs-japanese-cherry-trees-180950249/.

Time Life Magazine. *World War II: 100 Crucial Days: Key Events on the Path to Victory*. Wall Periodicals Online, 2015.

The U.S. Department of State, Office of the Historian. "Milestones: 1945–1952: Atomic Diplomacy." Accessed July 8, 2015. history.state.gov/milestones/1945-1952/atomic.

The U.S. Department of State, Office of the Historian. "Milestones: 1937-1945: Japan, China, the United States and the Road to Pearl Harbor, 1937–41." Accessed July 14, 2015. history. state.gov/milestones/1937-1945/pearl-harbor.

The U.S. Department of State, Office of the Historian. "Milestones: 1937-1945: Lend-Lease and Military Aid to the Allies in the Early Years of World War II." Accessed July 8, 2015. history.state.gov/milestones/1937-1945/lend-lease.

The U.S. Department of State, Office of the Historian. "Milestones: 1921–1936: The Neutrality Acts, 1930s." Accessed July 1, 2015. history.state.gov/milestones/1921-1936/neutrality-acts.

USO. "Our Organization: History." Accessed August 11, 2015. www.uso.org/history.aspx.

Ward, Geoffrey C., and Ken Burns. *The War: An Intimate History, 1941-1945*. New York: A.A. Knopf, 2007.

Warner, Brian. "How Rich Was Hitler and Who Gets His Mein Kampf Royalties Today?" Celebrity Net Worth. January 9, 2014. Accessed July 13, 2015. http://www.celebritynet-worth.com/articles/celebrity/rich-hitler/

Worthington, Jay. "Mein Royalties: Who Profits from Hitler's Bestseller?" *Cabinet* magazine. Accessed July 13, 2015. www.cabinetmagazine.org/issues/10/mein_royalties.php.

Yale Law School. "Three-Power Pact Between Germany, Italy, and Japan, Signed at Berlin, September 27, 1940." The Avalon Project. Accessed July 1, 2015. avalon.law.yale.edu/wwii/ triparti.asp.

JFK AND THE CUBAN MISSILE CRISIS

Andrews, Evan. (2014, July 28). "10 Things You May Not Know About Jacqueline Kennedy Onassis." History. July 28, 2014. Accessed July 28, 2015. www.history.com/news/10-things-you-may-not-know-about-jacqueline-kennedy-onassis.

CBS News. "1960: First Televised Presidential Debate." October 3, 2012. Accessed August 14, 2015. www.cbsnews.com/news/1960-first-televised-presidential-debate/.

Cosgrove, B. (2014, April 30). Behind the Picture: Photos From the Night Marilyn Sang to JFK, 1962. TIME. Retrieved August 17, 2015 from http://time.com/3879743/marilyn-monroe-john-kennedy-happy-birthday-may-1962/

Cuban Missile Crisis Shook Index. Historical Timeline 1959-1969.(2015). Dow Jones Industrial Average Learning Center. Retrieved August 14, 2015 from http://www.djaverages.com/

The Dow 1959-1969.(2015). Dow Jones Industrial Average Learning Center. Retrieved August 25, 2015 from http://www.djaverages.com/

Herbst, Diane. "21-Gun Salutes and Visits from JFK and Jackie: Inside the White House 'School' You Never Knew Existed." People. July 2, 2015. Accessed August 17, 2015. www.people.com/article/kennedy-family-photos-maud-shaw-white-house-school.

Hufbauer, Gary Clyde, Jeffrey J. Schott, Kimberly Ann Elliott, and Milica Cosic. "Case Studies in Economic Sanctions and Terrorism: Case 60-3 US v. Cuba (1960– : Castro)." Peterson Institute for International Economics. Updated October 2011. Accessed August 18, 2015. www.iie.com/publications/papers/sanctions-cuba-60-3.pdf.

John F. Kennedy Presidential Library and Museum. "13 Days in October." Accessed August 14, 2015. microsites.jfklibrary.org/cmc/oct16/.

John F. Kennedy Presidential Library and Museum. "The Bay of Pigs." Accessed August 20, 2015. www.jfklibrary.org/JFK/JFK-in-History/The-Bay-of-Pigs.aspx.

John F. Kennedy Presidential Library and Museum. "Cuban Missile Crisis." Accessed August 17, 2015. www.jfklibrary.org/JFK/JFK-in-History/Cuban-Missile-Crisis.aspx.

Life of Jacqueline B. Kennedy. John F. Kennedy: Presidential Library and Museum. Accessed August 17, 2015. http://www.jfklibrary.org/JFK/Life-of-Jacqueline-B-Kennedy.aspx?p=2.

McNamara, Robert S. "The Cuban Missile Crisis: Forty Years After 13 Days." Accessed August 21, 2015. www.armscontrol.org/act/2002_11/cubanmissile.

Metz, Robert. "$11 Billion Lost in Hectic Trading." The New York Times. November 23, 1963. Accessed August 26, 2015. www.nytimes.com/1963/11/23/archives/11-billion-lost-in-hectic-trading-market-closed-at-207-pm-volume.html.

Myre, Greg. "The U.S. And Cuba: A Brief History of a Complicated Relationship." NPR. December 17, 2014. Accessed August 18, 2015. www.npr.org/sections/parallels/2014/12/17/371405620/the-u-s-and-cuba-a-brief-history-of-a-tortured-relationship.

Olsen, A. J. Special to The New York Times. "Kennedy Pledges Any Steps to Bar Cuban Aggression," September 5, 1962. New York Times (1923–Current File). Accessed August 20, 2015. http://search.proquest.com/docview/116123114?accountid=5682

PBS. "Fidel Castro Timeline: Post-Revolution Cuba." Accessed August 20, 2015. www.pbs.org/wgbh/amex/castro/timeline/index.html.

Peace Corps. "History." November 20, 2013. Accessed August 17, 2015. www.peacecorps.gov/about/history/.

Radio and Television Report to the American People on the Soviet Arms Buildup in Cuba, October 22, 1962. John F. Kennedy: Presidential Library and Museum. Retrieved August 14, 2015 from http://www.jfklibrary.org/Asset-Viewer/sUVmCh-sB0moLfrBcaHaSg.aspx

Schlitz Brewing. "History." Accessed August 17, 2015. schlitzbrewing.com/.

Schwartz, Felicia, Jack Nicas, and Carol E. Lee. "Obama Administration Pushes for Deal to Start Flights to Cuba by Year's End." *The Wall Street Journal.* August 17, 2015. Accessed August 18, 2015. www.wsj.com/articles/obama-administration-pushes-for-deal-to-start-flights-to-cuba-by-years-end-1439860422#livefyre-comment.

Shabecoff, Phillip. "Market Activity Halted Abruptly." *The New York Times.* November 23, 1963. Accessed August 26, 2015. www.nytimes.com/1963/11/23/archives/market-activity-halted-abruptly-most-exchanges-stop-trade-minutes.html.

The U.S. Department of State, Office of the Historian. "Milestones: 1961-1968. The Cuban Missile Crisis, October 1962." Accessed August 20, 2015. history.state.gov/milestones/1961-1968/cuban-missile-crisis.

The White House. "John F. Kennedy." Accessed August 21, 2015. www.whitehouse.gov/about-the-white-house/presidents/john-f-kennedy/.

Walsh, Kenneth T. "The 1960s: A Decade of Promise and Heartbreak." *US News.* March 9, 2010. Accessed August 17, 2015. www.usnews.com/news/articles/2010/03/09/the-1960s-a-decade-of-promise-and-heartbreak.

THE VIETNAM WAR

Alpha History. "An American Draft Dodger Speaks About His Actions." June 16, 2018. Accessed June 18, 2018. alphahistory.com/vietnamwar/american-draft-dodger/.

American Experience. "Weapons of War: Aircraft, Transports, and Big Guns." PBS. Accessed September 9, 2015. www.pbs.org/wgbh/amex/vietnam/trenches/weapons.html.

Associated Press. "From the Archive, 29 April 1967: Muhammad Ali Refuses to Fight in Vietnam War." *The Guardian.* April 29, 2013. Accessed September 4, 2015. www.theguardian.com/theguardian/2013/apr/29/muhammad-ali-refuses-to-fight-in-vietnam-war-1967.

BBC On This Day. "August 25, 1967: 'American Hitler' Shot Dead." Accessed September 2, 2015. news.bbc.co.uk/onthisday/hi/dates/stories/august/25/newsid_3031000/3031928.stm.

Carland, John. "Office of the Secretary of Defense, Information Paper: When Did the Vietnam War Start for the United States?" United States of America Department of Defense. June 17, 2012. Accessed July 4, 2020. www.vietnamwar50th.com/assets/1/7/When_Did_the_Vietnam_War_Start_for_the_United_States.pdf.

CNN. "Clinton's Draft Deferrment." Accessed September 4, 2015. www.cnn.com/ALLPOLITICS/1996/candidates/democrat/clinton/skeletons/draft.shtml.

CNN. "Vietnam War Fast Facts." Accessed September 2, 2015. www.cnn.com/2013/07/01/world/vietnam-war-fast-facts/.

CNN. "Watergate Fast Facts." June 6, 2015. Accessed September 8, 2015. www.cnn.com/2014/01/23/us/watergate-fast-facts/.

Colagiovanni, L. (2012, July 26). Examiner.com. Retrieved September 4, 2015 from http://www.examiner.com/article/rush-limbaugh-dodged-vietnam-draft-due-to-a-boil-on-his-rear-end

Cooper, Michael, and Sam Roberts. "After 40 Years, the Complete Pentagon Papers." *The New York Times*. June 7, 2011. Accessed September 8, 2015. www.nytimes.com/2011/06/08/us/08pentagon.html.

Digital History. "My Lai Massacre." Accessed September 2, 2015. www.digitalhistory.uh.edu/active_learning/explorations/vietnam/vietnam_mylai.cfm.

Digital History. "Watergate." Accessed September 8, 2015. www.digitalhistory.uh.edu/disp_textbook.cfm?smtID=2&psid=3352.

Digital History. "Overview of the Vietnam War." Accessed August 13, 2015. www.digitalhistory.uh.edu/era.cfm?eraid=18.

Goldman, Russell. "Donald Trump's Own Secret: Vietnam Draft Records." *ABC News*. April 29, 2011. Accessed September 4, 2015. abcnews.go.com/Politics/donald-trumps-vietnam-draft-records-secret-documents-deferments/story?id=13492639.

Haberman, Clyde. *The New York Times: The Times of the Seventies: The Culture, Politics, and Personalities that Shaped the Decade*. New York, NY: Black Dog and Leventhal Publishers, Inc., 2013.

John F. Kennedy Presidential Library and Museum. "Robert F. Kennedy." Accessed September 2, 2015. www.jfklibrary.org/JFK/The-Kennedy-Family/Robert-F-Kennedy.aspx.

Kesby, Rebecca. "North Vietnam, 1972: The Christmas Bombing of Hanoi." *BBC News*. December 24, 2012. Accessed September 2, 2015. www.bbc.com/news/magazine-20719382.

Koroma, Salima. "The U.S. Doesn't Declare War Anymore." *TIME*. September 18, 2014. Accessed August 31, 2015. time.com/3399479/war-powers-bush-obama/.

Krogh, Egil. "The Break-In That History Forgot." *The New York Times*. June 30, 2007. Accessed September 8, 2015. www.nytimes.com/2007/06/30/opinion/30krogh.html?_r=0.

Latson, Jennifer. "The Other Pentagon Papers Secret: Few People Actually Read Them." *TIME*. June 20, 2015. Accessed September 8, 2015. time.com/3933636/pentagon-papers/.

LBJ Presidential Library. "LBJ: Biography." Accessed September 10, 2015. www.lbjlibrary.org/lyndon-baines-johnson/lbj-biography.

Maier, Eleanor. "The 'Gate' Suffix." *The Oxford English Dictionary* blog. Accessed September 4, 2015. public.oed.com/aspects-of-english/english-in-use/the-gate-suffix/.

McLaughlin, Kate. "Woodstock at 45: Still Stardust, Still Golden." CNN. August 25, 2014. Accessed September 9, 2015. www.cnn.com/2014/08/14/showbiz/woodstock-45th-anniversary/.

Military.com. "Famous Veterans: Jimi Hendrix." Accessed September 4, 2015. www.military.com/veteran-jobs/career-advice/military-transition/famous-veterans-jimi-hendrix.html.

Miller Center of Public Affairs, University of Virginia. "Lyndon B. Johnson: Key Events." Accessed September 22, 2015. millercenter.org/president/lbjohnson/key-events.

Miller Center of Public Affairs, University of Virginia. "Press Conference: July 28, 1965." Accessed September 10, 2015. millercenter.org/president/lbjohnson/speeches/speech-5910.

Moyar, Mark. "The Day That Turned the Vietnam War." *The Wall Street Journal*. October 31, 2013. Accessed September 1, 2015. www.wsj.com/articles/SB1000142405270230407320457 9169190447079968.

National Constitution Center. "26th Amendment: Right to Vote at Age 18." Accessed September 8, 2015. constitutioncenter.org/constitution/the-amendments/amendment-26-voting-age-set-to-18-years.

National Archives. "Pentagon Papers." Accessed September 3, 2015. www.archives.gov/research/pentagon-papers/.

President Lyndon B. Johnson's Biography. Lyndon B. Johnson Library. University of Texas at Austin. Retrieved September 22, 2015 from http://www.lbjlib.utexas.edu/johnson/archives.hom/biographys.hom/lbj_bio.asp

Rawlings, Nate. "Top 10 Abuses of Power: Richard Nixon's Plumbers." *TIME*. May 17, 2011. Accessed September 8, 2015. content.time.com/time/specials/packages/article/0,28804,2071839_2071844_2071846,00.html.

Readable. "Top 10 Famous People Accused of Draft Dodging." Accessed November 1, 2017. www.allreadable.com/fc27KkYk.

Rogers, Kenny. "Who Were U.S Presidents During the Vietnam War?" The Vietnam War. November 25, 2012. Accessed September 4, 2015. thevietnamwar.info/us-presidents-during-the-vietnam-war/.

Seelye, Katharine Q. "The 2004 Campaign: Military Service: Cheney's Five Draft Deferments During the Vietnam Era Emerge as a Campaign Issue." *The New York Times*. May 1, 2004. Accessed September 4, 2015. www.nytimes.com/2004/05/01/politics/campaign/01CHEN.html.

Selected Milestones of the Kennedy Presidency. John F. Kennedy. Presidential Library and Museum. Retrieved September 22, 2015 from http://www.jfklibrary.org/Research/Research-Aids/Ready-Reference/Selected-Milestones-of-the-Kennedy-Presidency.aspx

Selective Service System. "The Vietnam Lotteries." Accessed September 4, 2015. www.sss.gov/About/History-And-Records/lotter1.

Snopes. "Fact Check: Rush Limbaugh Avoided the Draft Due to an Anal Cyst?" January 25, 2015. Accessed June 13, 2018. www.snopes.com/fact-check/draft-notice/.

The U.S. Department of State, Office of the Historian. "Milestones: 1969-1976. Ending the Vietnam War, 1969–1973." Accessed September 2, 2015. history.state.gov/milestones/1969-1976/ending-vietnam.

The U.S. Department of State, Office of the Historian. "Milestones: 1961-1968. U.S. Involvement in the Vietnam War: The Gulf of Tonkin and Escalation, 1964." Accessed September 2, 2015. history.state.gov/milestones/1961-1968/gulf-of-tonkin.

The U.S. Department of State, Office of the Historian. "Milestones: 1961-1968. U.S. Involvement in the Vietnam War: The Tet Offensive, 1968." Accessed September 2, 2015. history.state.gov/milestones/1961-1968/tet.

The White House. "Richard M. Nixon." WhiteHouse.gov. Accessed September 2, 2015. www.whitehouse.gov/1600/presidents/richardnixon.

THE KENT STATE SHOOTING

Associated Press. "28 Deadliest Mass Shootings in U.S. History Fast Facts." CNN. Accessed October 23, 2015. www.cnn.com/2013/09/16/us/20-deadliest-mass-shootings-in-u-s -history-fast-facts/.

Buck, Stephanie. "The Weird, Rabid History of the Cabbage Patch Craze." Timeline. December 15, 2016. Accessed June 27, 2020. timeline.com/cabbage-patch-craze-867ce8d076c.

CBS News. "Fear Factor: How Herd Mentality Drives Us." October 19, 2008. Accessed June 27, 2020. www.cbsnews.com/news/fear-factor-how-herd-mentality-drives-us/.

Chan, Melissa. "Clown Sightings: Everything to Know About Clown Attacks." October 4, 2016. Accessed June 27, 2020. time.com/4518456/scary-clown-sighting-attack-craze/.

Little, Jane. "Mayan Apocalypse: End of the World, or a New Beginning?" *BBC News*. December 19, 2012. Accessed June 27, 2020. www.bbc.com/news/magazine-20764906.

Norman Rockwell Museum. "Norman Rockwell: A Brief Biography." Accessed June 29, 2015. www.nrm.org/about-2/about-norman-rockwell/.

Roach, John. "End of World in 2012? Maya 'Doomsday' Calendar Explained." *National Geographic News*. December 20, 2011. Accessed May 1, 2015. news.nationalgeographic.com/ news/2011/12/111220-end-of-world-2012-maya-calendar-explained-ancient-science/.

United States Census Bureau. "POP Culture: 1970." Accessed September 3, 2015. www. census.gov/history/www/through_the_decades/fast_facts/1970_fast_facts.html.

The U.S. Department of State, Office of the Historian. "Milestones: 1969-1976. Oil Embargo, 1973–1974." Accessed September 4, 2015. history.state.gov/milestones/1969-1976/ oil-embargo.

Yuhas, Daisy. "Psychology Reveals the Comforts of the Apocalypse." *Mind*. December 18, 2012. Accessed June 27, 2020. blogs.scientificamerican.com/observations/ psychology-reveals-the-comforts-of-the-apocalypse/.

WOMEN'S RIGHTS

Ali-Dinar, Ali B., Ph.D. (ed.). "Letter from a Birmingham Jail [King, Jr.]." University of Pennsylvania African Studies Center. April 16, 1963. Accessed March 7, 2018. www.africa.upenn. edu/Articles_Gen/Letter_Birmingham.html.

Bellis, Mary. "Top Inventions From the 1950s Through the 1990s." ThoughtCo. Updated August 21, 2019. Accessed September 9, 2015. inventors.about.com/od/timelines/a/modern_2.htm.

CNN. "1965 Selma to Montgomery March Fast Facts." Accessed September 1, 2015. www. cnn.com/2013/09/15/us/1965-selma-to-montgomery-march-fast-facts/.

Cohen, Sascha. "Why the Woolworth's Sit-In Worked." *TIME*. February 2, 2015. Accessed September 1, 2015. time.com/3691383/woolworths-sit-in-history/.

Cooper, Arnie. "An Anxious History of Valium." *The Wall Street Journal*. November 15, 2013. Accessed September 9, 2015. www.wsj.com/articles/SB10001424052702303289904579195872550052950.

FindLaw for Legal Professionals. "Roe v. Wade." Accessed September 3, 2015. caselaw. findlaw.com/us-supreme-court/410/113.html.

Holmes, Marian Smith. "The Freedom Riders, Then and Now." *Smithsonian Magazine*. Accessed September 1, 2015. www.smithsonianmag.com/history/the-freedom-riders-then -and-now-45351758/?no-ist.

IMDb. "Inspiration." Accessed June 26, 2015. www.imdb.com/title/tt0005551/.

John F. Kennedy Presidential Library and Museum. "Civil Rights Movement." Accessed September 1, 2015. www.jfklibrary.org/JFK/JFK-in-History/Civil-Rights-Movement.aspx.

Jones, Radhika. "Here's Why It's Been 29 Years Since a Woman Was Person of the Year." *TIME*. December 9, 2015. Accessed December 28, 2015. time.com/4141766/ time-person-of-the-year-angela-merkel-women/?xid=newsletter-brief.

Legal Information Institute. "Equal Employment Opportunity Commission." Cornell Law School. Accessed September 1, 2015. www.law.cornell.edu/wex/equal_employment _opportunity_commission.

Library of Congress. "The Civil Rights Act of 1964: A Long Struggle for Freedom." Accessed September 1, 2015. www.loc.gov/exhibits/civil-rights-act/civil-rights-era.html.

McLaughlin, Katie. "5 Things Women Couldn't Do in the 1960s." *CNN*. August 25, 2014. Accessed August 17, 2015. www.cnn.com/2014/08/07/living/sixties-women-5-things/.

National Archives. "The Civil Rights Act of 1964 and the Equal Employment Opportunity Commission." Last reviewed April 25, 2018. Accessed September 1, 2015. www.archives. gov/education/lessons/civil-rights-act/.

National Woman's Party. "Sewall-Belmont House & Museum." Accessed September 1, 2015. www.nationalwomansparty.org/visit.

Rielly, Edward J. *American Popular Culture Through History: The 1960s*. Westport CT: Greenwood Press, 2003.

Stanford University. "Major King Events Chronology: 1929-1968." Accessed September 1, 2015. kinginstitute.stanford.edu/king-resources/major-king-events-chronology-1929-1968.

Thompson, Kirsten M.J. "A Brief History of Birth Control in the U.S." Our Bodies Ourselves. December 14, 2013. Accessed August 17, 2015. www.ourbodiesourselves.org/ health-info/a-brief-history-of-birth-control/.

THE IMPENDING FALL OF DIAMONDS

Cape Town Diamond Museum. "What Is the Difference Between Real Diamonds and Synthetic Diamonds?" Accessed July 3, 2020. www.capetowndiamondmuseum.org/ blog/2018/06/real-diamonds-vs-synthetic-diamonds/.

Eschner, Kat. "Here's Why Pearls No Longer Cost a Fortune." *Smithsonian Magazine*. December 14, 2017. Accessed July 3, 2020. www.smithsonianmag.com/smart-news/ pearls-cost-fortune-180967540/.

Friedman, Uri. "How an Ad Campaign Invented the Diamond Engagement Ring." *The Atlantic*. February 13, 2015. Accessed July 3, 2020. www.theatlantic.com/international/ archive/2015/02/how-an-ad-campaign-invented-the-diamond-engagement-ring/385376/.

Gemological Institute of America. "Why Are Freshwater Pearls So Much Less Expensive than Akoya or South Sea Cultured Pearls?" Accessed July 2, 2020. www.gia.edu/ gia-faq-freshwater-pearls-less-expensive.

Guzman, Zach. "This Start-Up Is Selling Lab-Grown Diamond Rings at a 30% Discount and Jewelers Couldn't Tell The Difference." Make It. June 4, 2018. Accessed July 3, 2020. www.cnbc.com/2018/06/04/ada-diamonds-sells-lab-grown-diamonds-and-jewelers-cant-tell.html.

Luke, Amanda J. "Man-Made Diamonds: Questions and Answers." Gemological Institute of America. September 22, 2017. Accessed July 2, 2020. www.gia.edu/gia-news-research/manmade-diamonds-questions-answers.

Mia Donna. "Lab Grown Diamonds." Accessed July 3, 2020. www.miadonna.com/pages/stone-guide-lab-grown-diamonds.

Robbins Brothers. "E3 Diamonds: Lab-Grown Diamonds." Accessed July 3, 2020. www.robbinsbrothers.com/e3-diamond.

Sullivan, Paul. "A Battle Over Diamonds: Made by Nature or in a Lab?" *The New York Times*. February 9, 2018. Accessed July 3, 202. www.nytimes.com/2018/02/09/your-money/synthetic-diamond-jewelry.html.

Talmadge, Stephanie. "Lab-Grown Diamonds: They're Real, and They're Spectacular." GQ. October 16, 2018. Accessed July 1, 2020. www.gq.com/story/lab-grown-diamonds-are-a-thing.

THE RISE OF ARTIFICIAL INTELLIGENCE

1992: The Instant Language Translator. AT&T. Retrieved October 19, 2015 from http://www.corp.att.com/attlabs/reputation/timeline/92lang.html

Greenemeier, Larry. "Remembering the Day the World Wide Web Was Born." *Scientific American*. March 12, 2009. Accessed October 14, 2015. www.scientificamerican.com/article/day-the-web-was-born/.

Greenough, J. (2015, July 29). THE SELF-DRIVING CAR REPORT: Forecasts, tech timelines, and the benefits and barriers that will impact adoption. Business Insider. Retrieved December 29, 2015 from http://www.businessinsider.com/report-10-million-self-driving-cars-will-be-on-the-road-by-2020-2015-5-6

Kehoe, Brendon P. "The Robert Morris Internet Worm." MIT CSAIL. Accessed October 19, 2015. groups.csail.mit.edu/mac/classes/6.805/articles/morris-worm.html.

FIND A COACH

Badhwar, Neera K. "The Milgram Experiments, Learned Helplessness, and Character Traits." *Journal of Ethics* 13 (June 2009): 257–289. doi:10.1007/s10892-009-9052-4.

Explorable. "Milgram Experiment - Obedience to Authority." Accessed November 01, 2017. explorable.com/stanley-milgram-experiment.

McLeod, Sam. "The Milgram Shock Experiment." Simply Psychology. Accessed November 1, 2017. www.simplypsychology.org/milgram.html.

McLeod, Sam. "The Stanford Prison Experiment." Simply Psychology. Accessed September 3, 2015. www.simplypsychology.org/zimbardo.html.

NPR Staff. "Taking A Closer Look At Milgram's Shocking Obedience Study." NPR. August 28, 2013. Accessed September 9, 2015. www.npr.org/2013/08/28/209559002/taking-a-closer-look-at-milgrams-shocking-obedience-study.

Rogers, Kara. "Stanley Milgram: American Social Psychologist." Encyclopaedia Britannica Online. November 24, 2016. Accessed November 01, 2017. www.britannica.com/biography/Stanley-Milgram.

Romm, Cari. "Rethinking One of Psychology's Most Infamous Experiments." *The Atlantic.* January 28, 2015. Accessed November 01, 2017. www.theatlantic.com/health/archive/2015/01/rethinking-one-of-psychologys-most-infamous-experiments/384913/.

Stanford Prison Experiment. "The Story: An Overview of the Experiment." Accessed September 3, 2015. www.prisonexp.org/the-story/.

THE GULF WAR

Andersen, Kurt. "The Best Decade Ever? The 1990s, Obviously." *The New York Times.* February 6, 2015. Accessed October 19, 2015. www.nytimes.com/2015/02/08/opinion/sunday/the-best-decade-ever-the-1990s-obviously.html?_r=0.

Associated Press, Dow Diary. "Saddam Hussein's Invasion Helped Uncage a Bear in 1990." *The Wall Street Journal.* July 15, 1995. Accessed October 13, 2015. www.wsj.com/articles/SB837377710723383000.

Center of Military History: United States Army. "War in the Persian Gulf: Operations Desert Shield and Desert Storm August 1990–March 1991." Accessed July 4, 2020. www.history.army.mil/html/books/070/70-117-1/cmh_70-117-1.pdf.

Citino, R. "Technology in the Persian Gulf War of 1991." The Gilder Lehrman Institute of American History. Accessed October 15, 2015. https://www.gilderlehrman.org/history-by-era/facing-new-millennium/essays/technology-persian-gulf-war-1991

CNN. "Gulf War Fast Facts." July 28, 2015. Accessed October 15, 2015. www.cnn.com/2013/09/15/world/meast/gulf-war-fast-facts/.

Cold War Museum. "Fall of the Soviet Union." Accessed October 16, 2015. www.coldwar.org/articles/90s/fall_of_the_soviet_union.asp.

Gonzalez, Carolina. "President Bush Shows Houston to the World." *Houston Chronicle.* July 19, 2015. Accessed October 23, 2015. blog.chron.com/bayoucityhistory/2015/07/president-bush-shows-houston-to-the-world/.

Knott, Stephen. "George H. W. Bush: Foreign Affairs." Miller Center of Public Affairs, University of Virginia. Accessed October 2, 2015. millercenter.org/president/biography/bush-foreign-affairs.

Lawrence, John S. "The Persian Gulf Conflict and the Vanishing Hostages." *Journal of American Culture* 17, no. 1 (March 1994): 43–46. doi.org/10.1111/j.1542-734X.1994.00043.x.

Miller Center of Public Affairs, University of Virginia. "George H. W. Bush - Key Events." Accessed October 2, 2015. millercenter.org/president/bush/key-events.

The New York Times. "This Aggression Will Not Stand." March 1, 1991. Accessed October 5, 2015. www.nytimes.com/1991/03/01/opinion/this-aggression-will-not-stand.html.

Opposing Iraqi Aggression. American Experience. PBS. Accessed October 5, 2015. http://www.pbs.org/wgbh/americanexperience/features/bonus-video/presidents-policing-bush/

Schmitt, Eric. "Confrontation in the Gulf; Air Force Chief is Dismissed for Remarks on Gulf Plan; Cheney Cites Bad Judgement." *The New York Times.* September 18, 1990. Accessed

October 23, 2015. www.nytimes.com/1990/09/18/world/confrontation-gulf-air-force-chief-dismissed-for-remarks-gulf-plan-cheney-cites.html.

Transcript of News Conference Remarks by Bush on Iraq Crisis, August 6, 1990. *New York Times* (1923–Current File) Retrieved from http://search.proquest.com/docview/108495805?accountid=5682.

The U.S. Department of State, Office of the Historian. "Milestones: 1898-1992. The Collapse of the Soviet Union." Accessed October 16, 2015. history.state.gov/milestones/1989-1992/collapse-soviet-union.

The U.S. Department of State, Office of the Historian. "MILESTONES: 1989-1992. The Gulf War, 1991." Accessed October 2 2015. history.state.gov/milestones/1989-1992/gulf-war.

The U.S. Department of Veterans Affairs. "Public Health." Accessed October 15, 2015. www.publichealth.va.gov/exposures/gulfwar/sources/chem-bio-weapons.asp.

U.S. History: Pre-Columbian to the New Millennium. "The End of the Cold War." Accessed October 16, 2015. www.ushistory.org/us/59e.asp.

U.S. History: Pre-Columbian to the New Millennium. "Operation Desert Storm." Accessed October 2, 2015. www.ushistory.org/us/60a.asp.

Watson, Russell. "Crisis In the Gulf: War Path." *Newsweek.* August 26, 1990. Accessed October 21, 2015. www.newsweek.com/crisis-gulf-war-path-206032.

The White House. "George H. W. Bush." Accessed October 2, 2015. www.whitehouse.gov/1600/presidents/georgehwbush.

9/11 AND OTHER TERRORIST ATTACKS

9/11 Memorial. "September 11 Attack Timeline." Accessed. November 23, 2015 timeline.911memorial.org/#Timeline/2.

Associated Press. "Virginia Man Aided Hijackers, Lied to FBI About Further Attacks, Prosecutor Says." *Fox News.* December 6, 2001. Accessed July 4, 2020. www.foxnews.com/story/2001/12/06/virginia-man-aided-hijackers-lied-to-fbi-about-further-attacks-prosecutor-says.html.

CNN. "September 11: Chronology of Terror." September 12, 2001. Accessed November 23, 2015. edition.cnn.com/2001/US/09/11/chronology.attack/.

CNN. "Bush Declares War." March 19, 2003. Accessed August 28, 2015. www.cnn.com/2003/US/03/19/sprj.irq.int.bush.transcript/.

Davis, Marc. "How September 11 Affected The U.S. Stock Market." Investopedia. Sdeptember 2, 2011. Accessed November 9, 2015. www.investopedia.com/financial-edge/0911/how-september-11-affected-the-u.s.-stock-market.aspx.

Federation For American Immigration Reform. "Identity and Immigration Status of 9/11 Terrorists." Accessed November 4, 2015. www.fairus.org/issue/identity-and-immigration-status-of-9-11-terrorists.

The Federal Bureau of Investigation. "A Byte Out of History: 1975 Terrorism Flashback: State Department Bombing." January 29, 2004. Accessed September 9, 2015. www.fbi.gov/news/stories/2004/january/weather_012904.

Fox News. "Cheney: Order to Shoot Down Hijacked 9/11 Planes 'Necessary.'" September

4, 2011. Accessed November 23, 2015. www.foxnews.com/politics/2011/09/04/cheney-order-to-shoot-down-hijacked-11-planes-necessary.html.

George W. Bush. Presidential Library and Museum. "George W. Bush." Accessed November 17, 2015. www.georgewbushlibrary.smu.edu/en/The-President-and-Family/George-W-Bush.aspx

George W. Bush Presidential Library and Museum. "September 11, 2001." Accessed November 23, 2015. www.georgewbushlibrary.smu.edu/Photos-and-Videos/Photo-Galleries/September-11-2001.aspx.

The Gilder Lehrman Institute of American History. "George W. Bush on the 9/11 Attacks, 2001." Accessed August 28, 2015. www.gilderlehrman.org/history-by-era/facing-new-millennium/resources/george-w-bush-911-attacks-2001.

GlobalResearch. "9/11: When Did Cheney Authorize the Shoot-down of Civilian Planes?" January 21, 2015. Accessed July 3, 2020. www.globalresearch.ca/911-when-did-cheney-authorize-the-shoot-down-of-civilian-planes/5425959.

The Guardian. "Full Transcript of George Bush's Statement." September 11, 2001. Accessed November 23, 2015. www.theguardian.com/world/2001/sep/11/september11.usa19.

Lichtblau, Erich, and David E. Sanger. "August '01 Brief Is Said to Warn of Attack Plans." *The New York Times*. April 10, 2004. Accessed July 4, 2020. www.nytimes.com/2004/04/10/us/august-01-brief-is-said-to-warn-of-attack-plans.html?pagewanted=all.

Maranzani, Barbara. "9 Things You May Not Know About the Pentagon." History. January 15, 2013. Accessed November 2, 2015. www.history.com/news/9-things-you-may-not-know-about-the-pentagon.

McIntyre, D. (2007, January 9). Terrorism's Effects On Wall Street. Investopedia. Retrieved November 9, 2015 from http://www.investopedia.com/articles/07/terrorism.asp

National Commission of Terrorist Attacks Upon the United States. "Complete 9/11 Commission Report." Accessed November 2, 2015. govinfo.library.unt.edu/911/report/index.htm.

National Commission of Terrorist Attacks Upon the United States. "The Foundation of the New Terrorism." Accessed November 6, 2015. www.9-11commission.gov/report/911Report_Ch2.htm.

National Commission of Terrorist Attacks Upon the United States. "'We Have Some Planes.'" Accessed November 2, 2015. www.9-11commission.gov/report/911Report_Ch1.htm.

PBS. "Frontline: Fighting on Two Fronts: A Chronology." Accessed August 28, 2015. www.pbs.org/wgbh/pages/frontline/shows/campaign/etc/cron.html.

Ross, Brian. "While America Slept: The True Story of 9/11." *ABC News*. July 29, 2011. Accessed November 2, 2015. abcnews.go.com/Blotter/ten-years-ago-today-countdown-911/story?id=14191671#all.

Rudman, Warren. "Frontline: Why Did U.S. Intelligence Miss the September 11th Plot?" PBS. Accessed November 4, 2015. www.pbs.org/wgbh/pages/frontline/shows/terrorism/fail/why.html.

Sirota, David. "Under Fire From Donald Trump, Jeb Bush Focuses On 9/11 Even Though Hijackers Got Florida Licenses." *International Business Times*. October 19, 2015. Accessed

November 4, 2015. www.ibtimes.com/under-fire-donald-trump-jeb-bush-focuses-911-even-though-hijackers-got-florida-2146486.

Thompson, Mark. "U.S. Ends Its War in Afghanistan." *Time*. December 28, 2014. Accessed August 28, 2015. time.com/3648055/united-states-afghanistan-war-end/.

The White House. "George W. Bush." Accessed November 17, 2015. www.whitehouse.gov/1600/presidents/georgewbush.

COVID-19 & OTHER VIRUSES

Akpan, Nsikan. "New Coronavirus Can Spread between Humans—but It Started in a Wildlife Market." *National Geographic*. January 21, 2020. Accessed July 4, 2020. www.nationalgeographic.com/science/2020/01/new-coronavirus-spreading-between-humans-how-it-started/.

Allina Health. "Courage Kenny Rehabilitation Institute." Accessed August 5, 2015. www.allinahealth.org/Courage-Kenny-Rehabilitation-Institute/About-us/History/.

Barry, John M. "The Site of Origin of the 1918 Influenza Pandemic and Its Public Health Implications." *Journal of Translational Medicine* 2, no. 3 (January 2004). doi:10.1186/1479-5876-2-3.

Bloomberg News. "Why China's Deadly Viral Outbreak Couldn't Have Come at a Worse Time." January 22, 2020. Accessed July 4, 2020. www.bloomberg.com/news/articles/2020-01-22/china-s-lunar-new-year-nightmare-3-billion-trips-and-a-virus.

Campbell, Charlie. "Here's What It's Like in Wuhan, the Chinese City at the Center of the Deadly Coronavirus Outbreak." *Time*. January 22, 2020. Accessed July 4, 2020. time.com/5769323/wuhan-coronavirus-outbreak/.

History. "January 3, 1938: Franklin Roosevelt founds March of Dimes." Accessed August 10, 2015. www.history.com/this-day-in-history/franklin-roosevelt-founds-march-of-dimes.

Humphries, Mark Osborne. "Paths of Infection: The First World War and the Origins of the 1918 Influenza Pandemic." *War in History* 21, no. 1 (January 2014): 55–81. doi.org/10.1177%2F0968344513504525.

Influenza Strikes. The Great Pandemic: The United States in 1918-1919. United States Department of Health and Human Services. Retrieved on July 16, 2015 from http://www.flu.gov/pandemic/history/1918/the_pandemic/influenza/

Kosner, Edward. "Review: A World of Sickness." *The Wall Street Journal*. December 10, 2017. Accessed July 4, 2020. www.wsj.com/articles/review-a-world-of-sickness-1512938536.

McKay, Betsy, and Chao Deng. "First U.S. Case Reported of Deadly Wuhan Virus." *The Wall Street Journal*. Last updated January 22, 2020. Accessed July 4, 2020. www.wsj.com/articles/china-virus-kills-two-more-patients-as-authorities-step-up-control-measures-11579614626.

Smithsonian Natural Museum of American History. "Timeline: Whatever Happened to Polio?" Accessed August 5, 2015. amhistory.si.edu/polio/timeline/.

Statt, Nick. "Google Is Temporarily Shutting Down All China Offices Due to Coronavirus Outbreak." *The Verge*. January 29, 2020. Accessed July 4, 2020. www.theverge.com/2020/1/29/21113817/coronavirus-google-china-offices-temporary-closing-virus-outbreak-risk.

Trevelyan, Barry, Matthew Smallman-Raynor, and Andrew D. Cliff. "The Spatial Dynamics of Poliomyelitis in the United States: From Epidemic Emergence to Vaccine-Induced Retreat,

1910–1971." *Annals of the Association of American Geographers* 95, no. 2 (June 2005): 269–293. doi:10.1111/j.1467-8306.2005.00460.x

Vergano, Dan. "1918 Flu Pandemic That Killed 50 Million Originated in China, Historians Say." *National Geographic*. January 24, 2014. Accessed July 16, 2015. news.nationalgeographic. com/news/2014/01/140123-spanish-flu-1918-china-origins-pandemic-science-health/.

Wetsman, Nicole. "First Person-to-Person Transmission of Coronavirus Reported in the United States." *The Verge*. January 30, 2020. Accessed July 4, 2020. www.theverge. com/2020/1/30/21115402/coronavirus-us-transmission-person-to-person-first-case-re-ported-illinois-chicago.

Wetsman, Nicole. "World Health Organization Declares Global Public Health Emergency over Coronavirus Outbreak." *The Verge*. January 30, 2020. Accessed July 4, 2020. www. theverge.com/2020/1/30/21115357/coronavirus-outbreak-global-public-emergency -world-health-organization.

Yang, Stephanie, and Yoko Kubota. "Spreading Coronavirus Prompts Lockdown of More Chinese Cities." *The Wall Street Journal*. Last updated January 23, 2020. Accessed July 4, 2020. www.wsj.com/articles/spreading-coronavirus-forces-lockdown-of-another-chinese-city -11579774393.

FOUNDATIONAL READING

Andrews, Evan. "8 Reasons Why Rome Fell." History. January 14, 2014. Accessed November 25, 2015. www.history.com/news/history-lists/8-reasons-why-rome-fell.

Budiansky, Stephen. "Book Review: The Unkindest Cut of All." *The Wall Street Journal*. January 9, 2015. Accessed August 27, 2015. www.wsj.com/articles/book-review-the-killing -compartments-by-abram-de-swann-1420841846.

Constitution Facts. "Fascinating Facts about the Founding Fathers." Accessed December 8, 2015. www.constitutionfacts.com/us-founding-fathers/fascinating-facts/.

Death Penalty Information Center. "Early History of the Death Penalty." Accessed September 3, 2015. www.deathpenaltyinfo.org/part-i-history-death-penalty.

Digital History. "Overview of the American Revolution." Accessed November 30, 2015. www.digitalhistory.uh.edu/era.cfm?eraID=3.

Duignan, Brian. "Enlightenment." Encyclopædia Britannica Online. Accessed 30 November, 2015. www.britannica.com/event/Enlightenment-European-history.

The Editors of Enyclopaedia Britannica. "Mein Kampf: Work by Hitler." Encyclopedia Britannica. May 6, 2020. Accessed July 13, 2015. www.britannica.com/topic/Mein-Kampf.

The Electric Ben Franklin. "A Quick Biography of Benjamin Franklin." Accessed December 8, 2015. www.ushistory.org/franklin/info/.

Federal Trade Commission. "Our History." Accessed July 16, 2015. www.ftc.gov/about-ftc/ our-history.

Granger, Clive W. J. "Forecasting Stock Market Prices: Lessons for Forecasters." *International Journal of Forecasting* 8, no. 1 (June 1992): 3-13. doi:10.1016/0169-2070(92)90003-r.

Helliker, Kevin. "The Four-Minute High-School Mile, 50 Years Later." *The Wall Street Journal*. May 14, 2015. Accessed August 17, 2015. www.wsj.com/articles/the-four-minute-high -school-mile-50-years-later-1431643061.

History.com editors. "Punic Wars." History. October 29, 2009. Accessed December 17, 2015. www.history.com/topics/ancient-history/punic-wars.

Keim, Donald B. "Financial Market Anomalies." Wharton Finance. May 30, 2006. Accessed July 4, 2020. finance.wharton.upenn.edu/~keim/research/NewPalgraveAnomalies(-May302006).pdf.

Khan Academy. "The Rosetta Stone." Accessed December 2, 2015. www.khanacademy.org/partner-content/british-museum/africa1/ancient-egypt-bm/a/the-rosetta-stone.

Library of Congress. "The American Revolution, 1763-1783." Accessed November 25, 2015. www.loc.gov/teachers/classroommaterials/presentationsandactivities/presentations/timeline/amrev/.

The Metropolitan Museum of Art. "Washington Crossing the Delaware." The Met Collection Online. Accessed November 25, 2015. www.metmuseum.org/collection/the-collection-online/search/11417.

Nix, Elizabeth. "5 Things You Might Not Know About Julius Caesar." History. October 29, 2013. Accessed December 16 2015. www.history.com/news/history-lists/5-things-you-might -not-know-about-julius-caesar.

Purdue University. "Did You Know?: 'Washington Crossing the Delaware' painting." *Purdue Today*. February 13, 2014. Accessed November 25, 2015. www.purdue.edu/newsroom/purduetoday/didyouknow/2014/Q1/did-you-know-washington-crossing-the-delaware-painting.html.

Rotblut, Charles. "Investing Strategies for an Irrational Brain." American Association of Individual Investors. Accessed July 4, 2020. www.aaii.com/journal/article/investing-strategies-for-an-irrational-brain.touch.

Stanford Encyclopedia of Philosphy. "Aristotle's Ethics." May 1, 2001. Accessed August 31, 2015. plato.stanford.edu/entries/aristotle-ethics/.

U.S. History: Pre-Columbian to the New Millennium. "The Boston Patriots." Accessed November 25, 2015. www.ushistory.org/us/9c.asp.

U.S. History: Pre-Columbian to the New Millennium. "The Tea Act and Tea Parties." Accessed December 7, 2015. www.ushistory.org/us/9f.asp.

The White House. "George Washington." Accessed December 8, 2015. www.whitehouse.gov/1600/presidents/georgewashington.

Willis Tower. "An American Icon with a Rich History." Accessed September 3, 2015. www.willistower.com/building-information/history-and-facts/.

About the Author

Over his long investing career, Christopher Manske has helped many financial insiders and industry leaders to include Wall Street analysts, retiring investment advisors, and federal judges. A graduate of the United States Military Academy at West Point, Manske has been praised, published, or quoted in *The Wall Street Journal, Reader's Digest, U.S. News & World Report, Forbes, Financial Advisor Magazine,* and more.

As a successful money manager and business owner, he's enjoyed being a regular guest on both regional and national shows which can be heard via iTunes and iHeart Radio to include *The Jim Bohannon Show, The Ozarks Today, The Entrepreneur's Podcast Network, The Sales Whisperer, The Financial Quarterback,* and others. His thoughts can be seen online at *Yahoo! Finance, ThinkAdvisor, MSN.com, GoBankingRates.com, CEO World, Advisors Magazine, Home Business Magazine, Strategic Finance, Thrive Global,* and many more.

He was selected as a keynote speaker for the AARP and he and his team have addressed multiple companies such as Accenture and Boeing. Manske and his team have also worked directly with leaders at IBM, KPMG, GE, Microsoft, Exxon, and many others. Outside finance, Manske enjoys history and recently completed an award-winning restoration of a building originally built in 1910.